Everything Within

Alessandra Rizzotti
Shawn Sullivan

Neon Burrito Publishing
8 🎈

IRL: Los Angeles, California
URL: Neonburrito.info

Copyright © 2016 Alessandra Rizzotti & Shawn Sullivan

All rights taken.

isbn-10: 0692791108
isbn-13: 9780692791103s

HOMEGROWN (4)
&
Grief is a Process/
Growth is a Problem (68)

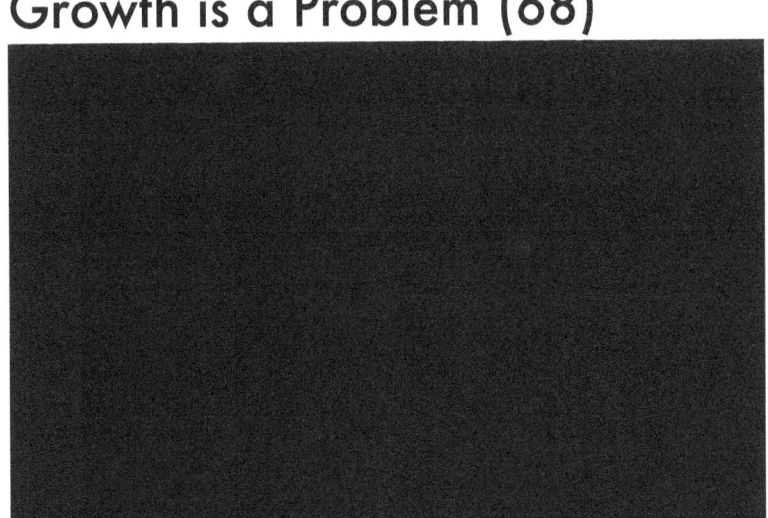

HOMEGROWN

florianne magdalena rizzotti
alessandra julia rizzotti
shawn sullivan (unrelated)

Florianne, Alessandra's grandma, taught herself how to write by reading Louisa May Alcott's *Little Women*. Through Alessandra sharing some of her poems on Instagram, Shawn left a comment asking her to work with him on this book.

Alessandra and Shawn live in Los Angeles but never talk IRL. Here's what a copyright looks like.

This is: feelings

My Whet - My Wit

Some people idlessly sit and chat-
I care not for that.
Others sit and knit-
Oh, I tried, I admit.
My whet is for meandering-
My wit is for philanthroping-
Many lifetimes have passed on,
Along with them, hours not born.
I love being me-
Ever so glad to be.
This being my train of thoughts,
My destination is now being sought.
Somewhere---who knows, where?

Sometimes---who knows, when?
Someone, who knows who---
Will find my lineage---
Their acquaintances

[Ed. Note: The poem Florianne wrote way back when that inspired us today to make this book and relate to each other through poetry.]

a preface of sorts

in the womb, my parents played mozart, and this i think gave me some sort of musical mind. i always thought in rhythms. when i was an infant, up until I was a toddler, my father would play Michael Jackson and "My Girl" and Stevie Nicks and we would dance, vigorously, rolling on the floor, somersaulting about. i found my personality in my feet, on the kitchen floor, sometimes dancing to "La Bamba" and Madonna, shaking my head to and fro, sassy. MTV was a huge influence and sometimes made me think i could be a pop star. i did impressions wearing midriff baring tops with polkadots and ruffles. i liked thinking i was the B-52s - as in, the whole band.

as for my mother's influence - i was born blue, cord wrapped around my neck. this says a lot about her, whose smothering tendencies frequently led me to fantasy games, making up dino and fairy stories in my crow's nest (not really a treehouse but it was a place to sit, on top of my swingset). i'd disconnect often in moments where she seemed she'd blow and this disconnection was very much a part of how i survived childhood. this was when i'd find paper and pen and write a lot. i once rewrote "Charlotte's Web" in pencil and crayon, but made it even more depressing, killing off Charlotte three times. then I wrote a novel in fifth grade about a girl who died on the Oregon Trail. she was like Anne Frank of the West, but she caused her problems by following a gold-studded dream to California, wrought with ground sloths. the computer game Oregon Trail inspired it. i illustrated a lot of it on Kid Pix but then decided that the tea-stained paper i hand wrote it on was more authentic.

i was singing opera at an early age, at first in front of the bathroom mirror, making up random gibberish Italian like words, then prayers in Hebrew School choir, then with a private coach who said i had potential to be something more, but i never believed it and when i failed at singing the solo and harmonies in "The Magic Flute," i sorta gave up and became tone deaf. except not really. i think it's still in me to sing, i'm just out of practice. i once got to sing a solo at Alice Telly Hall and really moved the judges. they mentioned me specifically. it was a song about brush strokes on a canvas, which by the way- i also dabbled in painting and pastels at an early age, mostly drawing farm animals, elephants, parrots, sometimes still life peaches, never straight lines.

but this was all after i was a child model and commercial actress. my mother really wanted to capitalize on my naturally curly hair at age three in order to raise money for college. she was the only working parent and it was a stress of hers to think of my future. so she made sure to curl every ringlet around her fingers, every day, dressing me in $80 fluffy European dresses, just to prove i was worthy of being on camera. which i was, many times. for example, i had to water a giant mechanical flower in the desert for a high-end Japanese dress commercial, then was in Rolling Stone Magazine posing as a flower girl for Fleetwood Mac (Fleetwood was in a wedding dress). i was almost cast in "In Living Color" singing "I Saw The Sign" by Ace of Base and i once spent a whole day eating cookies for a Pillsbury Doughboy commercial (it aired at the Academy Awards and paid for my braces). later i developed an unhealthy addiction to donut holes.

i was compared to Shirley Temple often. this was why i wrote an autobiography about her in the shape of a tap shoe for my second grade final project. i was also sometimes mistaken for a black child, playing Dorothy in "The Wiz," which is totally inappropriate, now that i look back on that. thankfully most of the musicals i starred in were Jewish interpretations of Disney movies (more appropriate). for Purim, we did a rendition of "Aladdin" and I was Jasmine, except really Esther, the Queen of Persia, who hid her Judaism and i don't really remember the rest, but this got the attention of a USC grad film student and he used me as a narrator for his film about Purim and its ties to the Holocaust. this sparked my interest in the idea of making movies, because i saw you could meld sound to visuals in totally mixed up ways and still come out with a story.

my mother and i watched movies (except cartoons) every weekend in the Century City AMC theater, now the Wakefield Plaza, eating Panda Express or In-N-Out illegally while the movies played, the plastic and paper rustling and making me embarrassed. i think "Batman" was my first movie. i cried and had to leave, though. my first name actually comes from the sound designer of "Rocky," who was actually named Alessandro, but they feminized it. "Rocky" is now my favorite movie, the first one that is. that and "Beetlejuice." for some reason i had a crush on Michael Keaton, but only in that movie. other influences included "Rainbow Bright" and "My Little Pony," just so you know how sophisticated i was. at least my neighbor Robin understood me when no one else would.

Robin was really imaginative. she made up stories about snow eagles and manatees and we would play every day, building forts in the house, going out to the backyard to make tunnels out of cardboard boxes. on Halloween, we'd cover the walls with trash bags and watch horror films all night under caves we constructed out of pillows. so, she was really the reason for my imagination. i even said so in my seventh grade essay about the most influential person in my life, which was her. she was the reason i got the 'best in creativity' and 'best in writing' awards in middle school, oddly enough for my poem "I Can, I Will." but, when she got sexual and started trying to get with every boy i liked, our games stopped and i lost trust in my creativity and found myself thinking i had to be practical about my future, which couldn't be in poetry, but instead filmmaking? somehow i thought that would lead me to a better career. and so i went to film school but i hated it and kept writing poetry and short stories and when a guy i was obsessed with said i was good at telling stories, i believed that writing was my thing. i should have believed it on my own, but didn't. that's probably why i keep trudging along in 9-5 jobs trying to make wages in things that don't make me happy. but i like health insurance and eating, and not having to live in the house that often gave me nightmares, the one where the womb almost killed me.

which brings me to the two times i almost died. the first time i was shaken almost to death in the Northridge earthquake. a bookshelf almost fell on top of me as i dove under a table to get shelter. and when we were all recovering from the trauma of this, when our gas stove was leaking and the foundation of our house collapsed, i temporarily started hanging at my friend Desiree's house, where i learned about the joys of swimming at night, getting pruny, then later taking hot showers with five shampoos and watching B movies - the ones set at summer camps that totally could have been softcore porn. she later had her dad cast me as a karate kid in the C-movie "Bloodsport II: The Next Kumite." it wasn't a SAG film, but i was SAG, so i had to lie to everyone that we flew to Thailand to shoot it. this was a ridiculous thing my mother made me do.

anyways, the second time i almost died was falling 60 feet off a cliff in Malibu. this is what led me to do standup in a neckbrace, telling jokes about being broken, which i was emotionally, too. i guess that all came from growing up without a dad, but who knows. i discovered i loved comedy until a man who loved me decided he wanted to make comedy his thing, and so i gently handed it to him like some kind of Chinese food takeout bag, which i shouldn't have, but that's ok, even though i am resentful, sort of, because he's not very good at it. you may have seen him getting eaten by a dinosaur in a movie. anyways, i later learned not to give pieces of my identity to men and now i write poetry or monologues and that is enough for me. except i'd also like to make an impact, maybe through the novel i'm writing about the mental health of my family. perhaps it will raise awareness about when to not have children. it's really all up in the air, though, what i do with the words i write.

but now, right now, just presently, death is looming in all my thoughts. as cancer grows in my father (a man i just reconnected with three years ago), i am grieving and processing it, and that is what has led me here, to tell bits of this story in this book, you may notice from time to time. i'm almost hoping for the sadness to be gone once my parents die, but that won't happen unless i make personal self-help life changes, which is an art of its own, a delicate balance of patience and acceptance of mysteries, learning that not everything is in my control, and that is ok. it is good.

Captain's Quarters

My old man didn't want it on the front door of his apartment
"It'll get unnecessary attention," he said
So I nailed it to the foot of his berth
A gold heavy metal sign that read
Captain's Quarters
Hoping that would give him
Dignity in his dreams
Maybe set him assail
But crevices in his bay
Collect dust
And the mast stands tall,
Empty coffee cans piling up
He builds the helm with cardboard boxes
Food with shelf life
Water bottles without caps
The masthead is made of premium macaroni
Gluten-free, tri-color veggie
He asked if I wanted to access
The escape hatch
Between the piles of newspapers
Science books
And baseball hats
From the starboard to the porthole
Where the sail got caught in the sickbay
We won't go to sea till he finds his feet

gimme a day to think about this, i'll tell you when the day is happening

thing is, i'm only mad at twelve days from this month so far
mmm, today's the thirteenth and who can guess what's ahead

although i must say, i'm tremendously pissed at my current day
days, you know, mad at my days
people -- i'm as sorry for them as they are for me,
that all this is happening
oh it's awful, so much drama, one grows tired of it eventually
if one doesn't grow tired of it immediately, which is typical

so i'm mad at my days, i'd rather not talk about it
the tide is pulled by the moon and that's how i am too

Moving Out

When we talk about how to divide the belongings
Light refracts from our prism
A rainbow appears
I detach
"You feel gone," I say
"I am still here," he says, hand to heart
Glowing white
His long legs dangle like spiders across the ottoman
I am holding a box of books, heavy like gold
Dust flies
I imagine shamrocks
The movers walk in
This will feel better when I have eaten Thai food takeout
He will drown his sorrows in the wine my brother bought us
"Why didn't you wait?" he asks
"I couldn't bare to see myself stay," I say
He says he will love me forever
Lucky to have known me for five years
My stomach sinks
The blinds close
The movers come in
"Is that it?"

Wake Up

In the morning
I normally hear the fan
Over everything
But today
An angry flock of seagulls
Fought over a parking lot
So rare in a city
Not by an ocean
It made me realize
That even if I wasn't
Where I wanted to be,
I could migrate anywhere
And still be unsatisfied

intense feelings when my eyes open

right away in the morning upon waking
life is a poem as a page in my head
(in my opinion)
mostly what's happening is
remembrances of a dream from my recent sleep
when i was able to love people who are gone from my life

Outside - Inside

                        I strapped seashells over my ears and back
                                    I wore them like armor
                It reminded me of when we were hermits
                          Fighting battles, clawing like crabs
                         Lately I feel like my skin is leather
               No man will find me beautiful unless 70,
           Drinking bourbon, wearing a Christmas hat
                                         It's not pleasing,
                    Swimming outside your houseboat

Age

1	2
In the front yard	And when I wanted
They cut a tree down	To feel big again
Not yet 100 rings	I plucked a leaf from another tree's branch
Ants would bury themselves to death	Held it up in the air
In the maple, squirming to feel again	And waited for the wind to
I took the trunk to sit on	Take me up
	Until it never did

Making Shadows in the Snow

Blustry winds have subsided,
Whirling snow has ceased-
Gray skies are now blue
The sun shines anew

This morning's hours are calm
The white snow is settled-
We stand and look about
It is a wondrous sight,
Making shadows in the snow

Shovels and brooms in hand,
We attempt to clear a path-
To reach busy streets
Making shadows in the snow

Alone

The chimes outside the kitchenette hanging by the hummingbird feeder put me in a dream and when I wake I feel the beating sunshine hit me red through the the stained glass windows on the neon floral couch- pink, green, yellow. It is the first time it feels like home. I crack the blinds to see the citrus- blood orange on the left- lemon on the right. I rest my feet in the cushion of the Persian carpet, my hands on the upright piano, sun hitting the top of my head as I let my voice direct the notes, or vice versa. I only let it last a few minutes until I hit the couch again, wishing someone would open the door and say, "I'm home, honey." But this quiet solitude is serenity and being alone isn't lonely.

in my soul there's a disco ball with facets of my memory

passing beyond family video's dark purple curtain
into the area reserved for people who want to get freaky
me and my cousin abby, who are like that, it's a family trait
we're kids headed into the horror and sci-fi vhs section
selecting ghidrah, the three-headed monster and son of godzilla
then packing ourselves in a car for a trip to lexington, kentucky
where my mother owns a dating business: matchmaker
international

at night in our hotel we hook our vcr to the tube, watch movies
vaguely aware godzilla is from the land of nintendo
then in the morning
while lexington begins its day outside our windows
inside we play rampage on
our hooked-up nintendo entertainment system

sitting in waldenbooks reading stephen king books, cousin abby
and i (visit the arcade sometimes) turn pages for hours until my
mother finds us
tells us long ago she asked security to look for "the boy with
long hair that's never combed... messy hair"

which happens years after the lexington hotel. happens when my
mother owns a retail store, chantilly lane, inside a mall, fairfield
commons, in beavercreek, ohio. here i spend days after middle-
school traveling back hallways, getting a kick out of the *super
mario 64* demo inside sears, stealing from claire's small stuffed
alligators, examining black-lights at spencer's, and considering
brookstone some kind of adult pleasure cove

then further into the future --
chantilly lane, which loses money, closes
same with matchmaker international
abby studies art in college, becomes a manager at chili's
marries and moves to louisville, kentucky
my mother sleeps on a couch in a friend's home in laguna beach,
california
up a hill facing the pacific
in los angeles alone in my bedroom i write a poem about abby,
godzilla
my mother, stephen king
etc.

xx

Bedroom

Mom painted the walls aqua and strung Christmas lights around the ceiling. Magenta, green, orange, blue. High school was for tactless creativity. A Chinese umbrella hung off in one corner, a European mask on the wall, a dollhouse I designed on a table against the wall, my Blink 182 collage on the door. It was "eclectic." "Unique." The glow-in-the-dark stars made me stay up at night. Sometimes I'd see ghosts or fairies on the ceiling, but really it was just the fire alarm blinking. At 5 am, mom would wake up to the radio, muffled words so loud against the stomp stomp of the step aerobics, I couldn't go back to bed till her shower would make me drift off in meditation but for ten minutes. And then it was my time to go to school, cold, hair still wet from the shower the night before, T-shirt clinging to my back.

then during the worst

while what's heavy pulls a person down
sinks a person
while the worst happens
still there are casual breezes on cool and quiet nights
tucked away from private narratives and
outside everyone's cerebral courtrooms
moments that mean nothing to the audience: i treasure them
no tragedy no message no meaning no way no how
by accident i find solace alone while wandering sidewalks
now and then
to here and there
perhaps with a good laugh at the end of this poem
us considering the possibility of cracking up right now
us deliberating the idea that everything is hilarious
ohhhh... if it were true!

Climate Change

The moon was
Burning pink-orange like a grapefruit,
Its size more sun-like,
Rotund, larger than normal
I thought the world was ending
While driving to my therapist's office
Because earlier that day,
A plastic bag full of lettuce
Burned up on the kitchen sink, smoking
Because the heat outside penetrated the window
Like a magnifying glass hitting an ant
And when I arrived
I felt the end of something
But wasn't sure if it was
Good or bad

Building for Two

you are a flower
in the crack of my driveway
the caulk
to a hole in my wall
i'd like to wallpaper your smile
to my room
plaster my hand to
your arm
sauder our hearts
into one

Booting Out Section A Residents to Buy Another Building

Let's lay down the facts
Two families
Must relocate
From one apartment
By tomorrow
Because the rent
Is doubling
And it's all my brother's fault
The question is
How do I tell family
That I don't believe
In their actions?
That what they're doing to their community
Doesn't align
With their love for me?

Boxes

My father has 193 cardboard boxes lining his apartment walls
"Insulation," he calls it
Thrown out of his storage unit
The boxes stay moldy, full of history
Box 125 has a hospital gown he wore during my birth
"These boxes are fire hazards," I say
They block passages we should be able to walk through
But he can't get rid of them because
Each one
Hoards memories
Giving him meaning
Giving me opportunities to learn more
There is order to the chaos, though
His inventory list is numbered and color coded
Boxes 25-29 are all memories from
When he was a tuxedo store manager in Beverly Hills
Dressing Maury Povich, Shaq, Michael Jackson
When he felt accomplished
When autographs served as recommendation letters
There is one VHS of me as a baby
And hundreds of photos of his mustache smiling
Then the photos get lonely in boxes 45-52
Because that is when he left
And didn't come back
There are more books than things
More paper clippings than letters
More hats and jackets than pictures
The true value exists in only four boxes
But I let him keep what he has because
This is the first time
He is not transient
The first time
Everything he owns
Is in one place

this excuse i have for feeling good sometimes i'm mentioning

club music
currently means a lot to my emotions

i listen to it frequently
though i haven't been dancing in clubs more now than in my past
as in i've barely gone to dance clubs at all
ever, they terrify me, and
my dance style
embarrassing!
i can't read the words in our universe's dance guidebook
and i wasn't born a dance god (ughck)

but i keep trying and lying, keep trying to tell everyone this:
imaginarily, i built my own invented dance style, it's
non-physical, complicated --

a bit tricky to explain
this dance in my head
which i perform for myself and others
regularly

and i can't turn myself into my dance's hologram on the floor
i got a glitchy hologram machine in my soul
that's too bad for both of us

i think about things like this while listening to club music
a.k.a. pop/electronic/dance music
which statement is verified by the fact
this poem is being written while i listen to
a club music playlist i assembled on spotify

(the writer maintains that the mentioned playlist
was present during all stages of this poem's
development, including its edit. for your information.)

battling against what brings one down
a.k.a. imagining a friend with whom i have this moment

1
yes, and...
mmm-hmm
...yup, totally...
[nods]
cool
...pages in my heart
sounds like...
....then, too...
[nods head]
i'm listening...

2
also there's the bad...
which i wanna fight against...
[stomps foot]
i try, everytime i see the bad, i try to fight it...
and...well, i agree
..fights don't always do good themselves...
i agree some fights become the bad
perpetuate it, help it endure...
feeling bad can be a bad fight against this world...
...so...when it exists for longer
i then try to fight it more...

3
i try to make the bad less
everywhere all the time always...i do ok...
no yeah, you're right about that...
pointless fights in my life have taught me
can't win a battle
that wasn't a battle in the first place
try to find the good fights worth having...
try not to let things
[whistles]
get me twisted, salty
or snotty

4
..sure, i'll have some lemonade...
great idea, thanks.
oh, things can get worse
and one can get stronger...
do you like dinosaurs?
let's chat for longer later.
if i don't help bring you down.
[claps]
any...you choose...
whichever you'd call your favorite dinosaur

let's not disturb productivity with feelings, but isn't talking about them productive, sometimes?

I feel at home talking about feelings
As in, my most serene place is in the feelings space
But that's not how I was raised
No, talking about feelings was not possible
With the 'rents
I feel at home talking about what traps me
Because all I want is to get it out
Leave it by the door
Like those charity letters with address labels
Like those flyers in Spanish about Jesus
Like those coupons for pizza takeout
But it's not like I would discard them, necessarily
Just gently let them know that I could let go of them
Maybe set them ablaze in a fireplace
That would be productive
To talk
Then let go
That's progress, right?
I would feel at home doing that
Not harping on the feelings
Just harpooning them
But let's not eat them up, ok?

i can't forget to remember

it isn't
it is
it isn't
it is

i had a thought

for a moment
and the thoughts
and the moment
are now gone
what good am i?

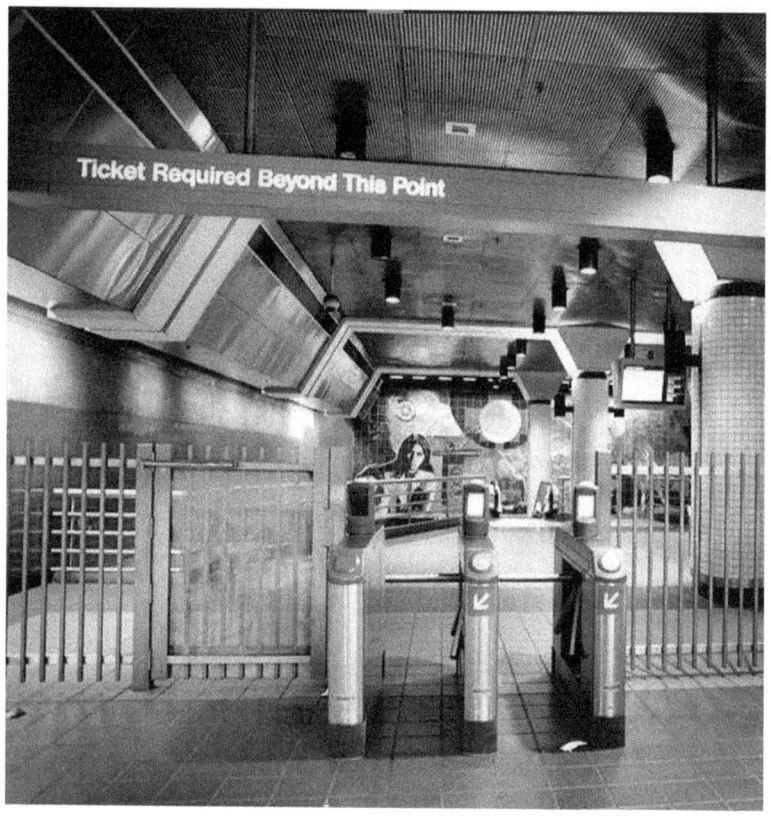

at night in los angeles

this city's fine to me however it is on whatever night we're talking about it's most exciting and works best for me when it behaves however it wants to behave

since anyway i picture all this everything happening (the world) as a tropical storm
and all one can do is picture everyone going through the same storm

i'm thanking you for my belief in others

there is love all around us
it's the sharing, that is most difficult
or so it seems
we accept the storms for what they are
we accept sunshine for what it is
we accept the rain for what it brings

inspired condolences

with the strength you endowed,
i managed to pass this day
my heart was heavy,
my head was a blur--
the yearning to "give up"
was great---
i murmured---this is it and i've had it---
but it was only me talking---
then i remembered how you
        tripped and fell-
across and walked again
the cross you carried
        added to your plight-
they didn't know wrong from right-
upon you dying
you gave me birth,
i'll face tomorrow without self sorrow,
believing in you, i'll carry on-
trusting in you, i can't go wrong

wind

trying so hard
to blow you
to non-existence

i am real

i am alive
i have the duty to perform
just being me

perplexing incidents in life that are, in fact, unremarkable and potentially wonderful

can't remember if it was a microscope or a telescope -- i think it was a periscope
not much of a scientist, though i find it all quite fascinating
visit nationalgeographic.com every day
and i can't recall if i used a microscope or a kaleidoscope or a gyroscope
a stroboscope or an oscilloscope, perhaps a stethoscope
oh, oh, oh. i remember now it was my horoscope

off topic:
I dream of utopia because of course i dream of paradise
dystopias are to me redundantly the worst of now and always
you imagine the worst as lasting forever, you do that
may it be that the sun one day cracks through your clouds
and piercing sunshine gives energy to your ground for life and birth
but if not, well
i recommend regularly watching post-apocalyptic movies for reminders
to stay strong and kind during hard times

hands up

hands up-
        what are we going to do this morning
        what are we going to do with our hands?
shall we play the piano? plinky tinkle tee
or the drums? baromp baromp baromp
or the flute? deedly deedly dee
oh oh oh oh hands up-
        what shall we do?
shall we paint a picture? slip slip sloop
or model with clay? clip clap clop
or cut with scissors? snippity snippity snip
oh oh oh oh hands up-
        what shall we do?
we think it is wise, to start the day
with folded hands and pray
thanking god for our safety
thru both day and night
thanking god for our caring
so we may, in this way

        start our day

        hands up

(maybe i'll make this into a book or song)

        i dislike being called a

        non-professional
        good homemakers
        are few

Boyle Heights

This is a city of immigrants
Even the whales that were here first came from somewhere else
The mastodons moved them out, a gentrification of the ocean
That eventually became concrete
WW2 brought the Jews and Japanese, replaced by Mexicans
Mariachi uniforms
Lamb stew
Street tacos
From movie theaters to jean shops
Shuls to galleries
Department stores to vacant lots
An identity crisis influx
My brother wouldn't live here
But I most certainly would
It's just the white washing I can't accept

excerpts of a letter

Torrential, not the word
Fiercely off on rain
Gallons and gallons
Flooding the streets
Rushing past our domain
To settle where the cars were parked
And appear to be floating

on the other side of the phone

he seems happy
younger
the smile is there
even in the hospital
because he's on
zoloft
cancer meds
pain relievers
and took a dump

i am skeptical, though
of the healing
how long will it last
till he needs me
to lift him
from his chair
change his diapers
pull on T-shirts and elastic pants

last week he held my hand
for the first time in twenty-two years
it was a weak grip
in the Walgreens
as I changed his Depends

i want more
but that could have been it
his death day might be the same year
as Leonard Nimoy's

the neighbor kid

digging a hole in the front yard
with the front of his skateboard
i asked what he was looking for
"gold," he said.
but the dirt was hard, impenetrable
not even flowers could grow there
i gave an encouraging nod
"good luck"
later he pulled out a rock
with a gold spec
the other kids in the neighborhood crowded around
this was their answer
he was their hero

since this conversation won't in reality take place between us

like when a neighbor leaves on their alarm(!) clock
without them realizing they did, and while they're gone their noise persists
punctures my silence, keeps me awake, pesters me

my emotions have been like that in my body while i've been alone
a ringing alarm that disquiets my days, troubles my thoughts
with no one emerging to switch the alarm off and i can't reach it myself
--
a window was tried, turned out to be ridiculous, too shy to call a locksmith

wanna repeat: no one's coming to turn the alarm off
such was told to me one day in a car ride that happened by dumb luck
pure knotty chance and a cemetery atmosphere
by matter of simultaneous, unrelated objectives for each person's day
on a morning well after our first goodbyes
she told me returning to me would be moving backwards for her
she reminded us of my imperfections, spoke of her current happiness
what first made me feel better is i've seen british movies with this theme
here's the theme: the living reality of being human and how terrible that is
gripping stuff dramatically, outrageously normal, happens to everyone
which is both exactly true and a little off. tolstoy wrote about it:
anna karenina, which says "each unhappy family is unhappy in its own way"
but still people think they know how others hurt, i.e. not enough people read

back to what i was saying: by the curb in front of my place
a dark crystal shard of me was hung beneath her rearview mirror
we wondered what behind us and within me is even worth a damn
then she told me, during the afi film festival which we'd gone to together
in fact she'd printed my tickets
(this was before thanksgiving when she met my sister and nieces)
she met a guy who is what she wants and needs

my emotions that day/today: absurd, incomprehensible
this felt/feels to me as bad as it sounds
destined for hyperbole in my emotions
this gothic story clinging as a gargoyle inside me

of the ex-girlfriends who live in my heart there's now one ghost

i remember when you sneezed on a cat.
quiet running in hotel hallways at night.
fante's terrific opening line: "It was a bad one, the winter of 1933."
the play section of bookstores because those people understand pageantry.
anytime anybody gets to be calm and mellow driving streets listening to their favorite music.
scientists who provide emotional explanations for their field of study.
the neighborhood outdoor cat, this orange and white domesticated chiller badass on hayworth day and night.
the fact that f. scott fitzgerald died outside a home on hayworth.
splashes of neon and more from more and other bright artificial city lights that give a clear fake glow, bulbs and glass as the sun in a day, but more laid back since it's imaginary and i prefer the quietness of nights, the swaying of palm trees and the moon being in some type of shape or whatever, plus everything not being mentioned.
situations involving trips to farms (bonus: animal encounters).
anybody who can whistle the song i can't remember the name of, then provide the name of the song, then invite me to their house on sunday where we'll eat pretty solid bbq food and have an alright day together.
i adore kmart realism and people who unadore kmart realism.
sounds like it sounds as it feels like it feels while it's happening.
little tokyo in downtown los angeles, especially community karaoke outside the grocery store in the courtyard and this area's second-floor restaurant with its happy hour menu.
goodbye blue monday, revisiting vonnegut, kilgore trout being from dayton ohio, sturgeon's law of 90% crap.
thinking about the san andreas fault while watching manglehorn at the sundance theater on sunset, feeling for a moment like my seat is trembling, which causes me to wonder if an earthquake is happening but actually it turns out everything is ok and i don't need to worry about this right now.
i have trouble trusting a person who won't eat at a diner with me.

seek the truth and nothing but the truth

as the reflection of nature's grandeur is captured by the still water, so too is a glimpse of infinity captured by a still mind

but i worry

i made him out to be someone really intellectual and strong and exciting in my mind
someone who could lift me up while waxing on about foraging for mushrooms and peddling organically churned ice cream on a handmade bamboo bike
which sounds ridiculous, i know
but it's a fantasy
that makes the reality just plain and boring
the usual
i think of someone as having a hyphenated career like "psychologist of chroma-experience-design" with interests like "invisible street art"
and then it turns out they're unemployed and don't believe in hard work
i expect them to fulfill the expectations i had of myself
so the hole that exists in me becomes deeper,
a grave full of ramps, which i hear are incredibly rare raw garlic scallion like things worth $40 a pop, like a truffle
these rarities, these fads
makes me want to simplify
but i keep searching, keeping others at bay
i gotta laugh at the Harvard Columbia Princeton Brown crowd
because who do they think they are?
i mean, really?
their world isn't reality,
propped up by parentals, moneybag foundations
i can't deny, though, they make me feel real small
and then i want more of what they have
just to have it
which makes me smaller
a never-ending loop
but maybe they'd get a kick of that
me, my brain
i could be their clown, no?
a trained-in-Paris anaerobic mime with ASL skills and aspergers?
they'd like all the elements
it'd be a good TED "talk"

a note on murakami

impresses the hell out of me how murakami smoothly portrays wildly flawed characters
e.g. when tsukuru is flatly denied further physical intimacy with a woman since
as she explains to him
he has emotional issues and doesn't act like a grown up

there's a larger story to a murakami book than the characters' little problems
yet not large enough to find truth and answers and reality
since fiction is like memory and vice versa
anyway there's the entirety of tsukuru's pilgrimage
even while he dwells on topics particular to him
his life's topics accumulate into a book-sized story
i like it, i can relate, and i like how the book is chatty and human

then this: my life into art and art into my life

"... grateful that what had taken hold of his heart was a deep sorrow, not the yoke of intense jealousy."

it's to me as if a pen somewhere put the scene together:

going down the sidewalk to see *angst* (indeed)
(which movie i'll later discover is sold out) with my headphones on
i walk past her and her boyfriend, whose spirits don't look too high
and i can't know their reasons (ticket woes?)

it's the first time i've seen her since our goodbye in her car
she's looking down as we pass, i don't know the guy but i'll say he's a human
i'm listening to neutral milk hotel, reflecting on what
i'd known would happen having happened

so, without the movie i seek union with a book, which often i do
reading more murakami, i'll be damned -- on the pages i read tsukuru
passes a girl (the girl from my above note about murakami)
with another guy on the sidewalk (!!!) confirming his reputation:
murakami somehow reads inside me

"People come to him, discover how empty he is, and leave. What's left is an empty, perhaps even emptier, Tsukuru Tazaki, all alone."

[futuristically altered] four lines i saved on my phone's notepad one day while walking

the song of how weak you are is toneless and tired
how strong you can be is some of my favorite music
be strong when you tell me how weak you are
strong and light despite what's weak

the theory 15 years ago

I knew it to be cancer
Leave well enough alone
If it is and is exposed to air
The end is near
Cancer can consume
Does consume
Doctors heed
"Cancer can arrest itself"
Leave well enough alone

july 20, 1980

If you are doing excellent
You got the spirit

Within you
Psychosis spreading
Twas a bit after eleven
Restless was I
Walking back and forth
Nobody to talk to
But I heard
Sauntering stairways
Heaven shedding tears

parents,
better you should have your children on your back then have
children without backbones

people and their problems, all just convoluted thought processes

I'm sick of it all
People and their insecurities, their resentments
Wondering what he's going to say
What she should say
Why he's doing that
How it's all going to work out months from here
Will it work out at all
She did this to me
He did that
All this talk
Doesn't seem worthy of my time
When the solution could be
Not worrying at all
Or just making a phone call
Sorting it out in a two sentence email
Stating exactly what wanted to be said
Stopping the wondering
Communicating not around the issue, but towards it
Or maybe the solution is not thinking about the shoulds and always
Don't get me wrong
I've been what annoys me
But recent deaths and illnesses
Keep me away from the negative thought processes
I'd rather drink a hot chocolate
Go to the spa
Turn on chi activation sound waves
Sleep it off
Till tomorrow
But of course I too go to a dark place, sometimes
Cleansed with tears
It happens less often with therapy
It happens less often in solitude

you think you have troubles?

don't take it lying down
get up and fight!

my rosetta stone

to begin in my furthest future, at my funeral, it should either be that tom waits performs "tango til they're sore" or someone plays that song off their phone from youtube, at least (request of mine)

except, not dead yet -- so, as a child in ohio i hold a stuffed-bear wearing a hawaiian shirt (the bear was wearing that shirt) and watch cartoons alone in an apartment living room on a saturday before my mother and sister wake. my summary of me: i think my life is nonsense and cartoons are reality

the bear's giver marries my mom. we move into his house. it has a family room, with a wood-cased tv he built. i watch vhs tapes of *the three stooges* and *e.t.*, *inspector gadget* on nickelodeon. my stepdad, who works for the air force, his curiosities then are classical music and cd technology. i become familiar with both the german way to pronounce "w" and physical media of the future

after my mother's business's financial success, my family moves into a large house freshly built in the country. in my own big room i have an old tv, then i have an old tv and a new tv from wal-mart. in this environment formative years occur while i read r.l. stein, watch cartoons on nickelodeon, then cartoon network, then movies off hbo and tnt (which i tape onto vhs, e.g. *serial mom*, *red rock west*). often at night after-news sitcom reruns play on my old tv while i videogame on my new tv, sometimes while music drifts from a stereo above my dresser, except music distracts and it depends on the show/night, but definitely sometimes my bedroom and heart swelled from music. through my teenage sister i hear nirvana and weezer, but the *pocahontas soundtrack* and kris kross are my choices, then mtv a.k.a "video killed the radio star" (sidenote: learned about this song from *the wedding singer soundtrack*) from the country home, following my high-school years, my mother and i live in an apartment on sally circle. fleeing from the world and oblivious about how to chase it, i become magnetized by movies, e.g. *city of god*, *live flesh*. i listen to emotional teenager music, e.g. the promise ring, american football. at one point i tell a friend i want to make a movie that's a cross between *the rock* and *face-off,* then after a few years i tape an antonioni quote† above my tv written in pen on notebook paper. i read biskind's *easy riders, raging bulls* and gilbey's *it don't worry me*, talking also about movies with my manager, which manager of a second-run theater graduated majoring in film from local wright state university. he chats with me about sam peckinpah, robert altman and classic universal horror movies. one midnight for only us three after the business closes, his friend brings over his *horror of dracula* 35mm print, i have my first repertoire film experience with them (plus i'm drunk from vodka in a plastic water bottle and sneak a cigarette in the theater with my manager)

before our things arrive in laguna niguel, california, i read kerouac's *on the road*, watch a rented *the last temptation of christ* dvd on my pc. i come to southern california because of dreams i have about movies. my mother says she's dreamt of living here since her childhood. we are the classic country family moving to california setup: we have little money, make little money, and everything looks interesting/amazing while we feel confused/excited. a year after various changes in my california setup, including buying bukowski books while alone, then arrive short and treasured days in a long beach loft with two friends. then a pal of mine, also interested in movies, moves from ohio. we nestle into a one-bedroom apartment in mission viejo, both go to saddleback college. his parents pay our rent. i work at costco. we watch movies on his tv and drink liquor while listening to music during long hours of our days together

---

† "And here we witness the crumbling of a myth, which proclaims it is enough to know, to be critically conscious of ourselves, to analyze ourselves, in all our complexities and in every facet of our personality. The fact that matters is such an examination is not enough."

at this age i devote my personal time to movies, music, and, especially after my pal and i stop getting along, i read books. alone in a laundry room i read *if on a winter's night a traveler.* in film classes, i make friends who see the world through movies as i do. keystone moments arrive relating to *un chien andalou* and *v for vendetta*. in the arts i feel myself growing. my pal and i decide not to live together past our one-year lease. while living with my mother again in the same apartment as when we arrived, at school i become friends with a serious book person. he introduces me to the writing of david foster wallace, then i read *infinite jest*, which was a thing people who were interested in books might be doing in those days. it takes me a year to read it, since i begin by multi-reading (e.g. *geek love*, a favorite of mine), then i pause for nine months, reading other things, e.g. *all the king's men*, *invisible man*, and after i sit down and finish *jest*, i then read vonnegut's *slaughterhouse-five* and thompson's *the rum diary* in two days, since it's much easier to read other books after finishing d.f.w.

except that's skipping ahead, since i make friends while living with my mother, but i finish *jest* while living in brentwood, with my girlfriend who's interested in books and movies and music too. 75% of my current favorite horror movies i first watch with her. we move to portland, oregon, where i go to the northwest film center, becoming friends with my editing teacher, who teaches me more about film from the '60s and '70s and modern global cinema. in his studio apartment he shows me *the holy girl*, *morvern callar*, *innocence* -- movies from different perspectives (his favorite is female) and he likes when there's a bit of serious fun involved in art, calls himself hedonistic, likes cooking. a favorite movie of his is *withnail and i*. once in a theater he rented, we changed into costumes during metzger's *score*

i go to movie theaters whenever there's an excuse to go. i binge the portland international film festival. i haven't figured out the adult world at this juncture. i burn savings from my days at costco. motivated by my serious book friend, who lives in portland (a reason it was chosen), during the day i read often. i regularly visit the central library and sit at the big wooden community table with whatever i'm carrying: novellas e.g. *senselessness, the invention of morel*, big ones e.g. *the brothers karamazov, 2666*, normal-sized e.g. *the rings of saturn, ask the dust.* etc. this is a pivotal period in my life in terms of my adventurous inquiries into theories and curious personal practices. a blending of my plural dreams into my singular reality within portland during these two years of my life on the fringe of things that matter

many nights my girlfriend and i cuddle, watch 1-3 movies on the blu-ray player attached to the lcd tv i bought when costco cashed out my vacation hours. pre-code movies, movies from hong kong, romania, france, japan, the silent era, mondo macabro, criterion, new home theater releases -- mostly through netflix and redbox (hollywood video on our street's corner had shuttered). then my girlfriend and i split up, so i transition back to los angeles, first staying in my sister's guest house reading tortilla flat (and texting my reader friend about this, which friend texts me no longer these days), then sleeping on a friends' couch reading a copy of *sandokan.*, then life, more life, *goodbye to language 3d*, etc.

the above (and below): a colossal abridgment! skipped my nights of drinking peppermint schnapps in a laguna niguel garage, listening to magnolia electric co. and wanting to die. in a separate story from this same garage, i orgasm during the white album's "long, long, long". life beyond death. i see *killer of sheep* at the billy wilder theater while living with friends in westwood, happens. oh it should be said, during a rewind, that important changes in my development occurred when my mother, from jungle jim's international market's dvd department, purchased *rebels of the neon god, god's comedy, il postino* and other movies she thought seemed interesting maybe, and they did tend to be i thought, when i watched them in the kent state university dorm i shared with my pal, at which school i was a weekly news cameraman and film club attendee my aunt has said to me before that she believes my path toward artistic endeavors relates to her and my mother taking me and her daughters to plays at the victorian theatre in our youth. my internship at a black-owned black-tv station in dayton ohio sounds instrumental. costco: pizza kitchen to tire department. crucial night: friend showing me *night on the galactic railroad*. buying cheap dvds from bins at wal-mart and best buy: bringing it up. *the skulls* was the first pirated movie shared with me <- noted.

my father (who's never been married to my mother nor lived with her) used to play me old radio programs (superman, gangster drama) off cassettes when i went to sleep while visiting him. he bought me my first nintendo entertainment system, which he kept at his place, in order to sharpen his mario talents. though i first fiddled with a nintendo in the country basement of my cousin who once while playing *skate or die* showed me his pubic hair to demonstrate what growing up is like. he had an alanis morisette poster in his room. his sisters watched nickelodeon as often as i did, since we'd watch snick together at my grandmother's house on saturday nights, back when grandmother was alive and much of the family lived in ohio, before my first ohio departure when i lived in michigan for one year

my earliest vivid memory of seeing through the arts a world which my dreams desired to inhabit comes from inside books & co. during my youth. bet i was there to check on new *fear street* releases, when i noticed on a holiday endcap a book's cover painting of a lonely house with candle-lit windows, snow on its roof, snow on the ground. i dreamt of living as happily as i felt while looking at that cover then, imagining myself safe and comfortable in that home, for some reason, that sounds kinda funny and it's an example of one of the biggest things that's happened to me during my construction into who i am today, and i remember i was drinking a glass bottle of strawberry sparkling water from the bookstore's cafe

the problem with going to my childhood home, you see

it's not the discomfort
or maybe it is
i'm trying to put my finger on it
it's a combination of soothing and painful
like what cutters think of cutting
like the second degree burns i give myself in the hot shower
i want to feel at home in my home
but it ends up feeling like a mousetrap
cheese, then snap!
so i avoid it
i only go to the backyard occasionally
to check on the bees
making sure to suit up
wearing leather to protect my hands
but i gotta admit
i love a good sting
it's the only way to feel
anything
i heard Ron Swanson say on 'Parks and Recreation'
not to mistake drama for love
even though that's all i know
with pain, comes pleasure
but i gotta clear myself
of those vibrations
it's time to find
a better match
my therapist says it will never happen
unless i cut my mother out
makes me want to burn my childhood down

but what if i never find the person

i really want that high
that compatibility high
something about being with someone
that seems so nice   *most times*
exciting
if not real   a heart is cautious
but totally faded   and there are many reasons
if drawn out   "why"
never a happy middle   but i liked you
i should do a lot of digging   (snap your fingers)
through the rolodex   just like that
inside myself   cause "you are you"
maybe i'll get to finding later   and "i am me"
but that's such a cliche journey
and i don't want to do it
because it works

when the daughter of the ex-boyfriend calls the ex-girlfriend

i am letting her know that her ex-love is dying
i decided to do this so that
she could have closure
but who am i to decide that?
i guess i just wanted to know how she felt
i think he still loves her and wishes they were together
he has a picture of them
"getting married" in a Coke commercial
sitting by his bed
she is sending him a note today
i wonder what it says
she is sending me pictures
i wonder what i'll see
what if he dies
before the note gets there?
what if the closure between them never happens?
i just want to know that he is capable
of loving still
if not with me

when friends go away to the families they create and no one is left, but that's just an exaggeration because i'm depressed

the reasons i'm staying in this city
are all just fabricated excuses
if i leave, i won't have friends anymore
all my friends are here, after all
but they're all getting knocked up
so i rarely see them anyways
if i leave, i won't be near my doctors
and i'll become more paralyzed without them
but there are doctors everywhere, really
if i leave, i am a coward
not facing myself
because if i leave, my problems follow
but these are all ifs
so i shouldn't be concerned, really

Webster Says:

Trustee:
a person or institution to whom property is turned over to be managed for the benefit of others

Custodian:
a keeper, guardian, relating to custody
(custody=imprisonment)

Survivor:
a legacy depending upon survival

Anthony*:
I'm praying your salary increase is coming from the "state lottery" because I'm an artsy homeowner.

today is the day i'm thinking about this

at first all i knew and what he'd told me is we couldn't be friends, and by asking another friend to ask him about this situation is how i heard it's because i was a well poisoner
that's all i heard, so both me and the person whom he'd told wondered what that meant
at this age i'd never had someone stop being friends with me, i was in my mid20s

i'd never before had someone call me a well poisoner
these years later i have two (solid?) guesses about what he meant

i'm a well poisoner since i'm most used to and sometimes seek emotions of despair
(since i desire emotions and it's always easier to find the bad)
a problem here is if i notice someone else's happiness i can mistrust it
i can say the universe is telling me to do it
i can say in a universal sense there isn't a reason to be happy during the current moment
i can say that, thinking what's happening doesn't matter ultimately
i'll think it doesn't matter and i won't even notice i'm being an asshole
and tones of distress are never ones that people seek to be around

or, he just meant i was a well poisoner for having someone ask him about our situation
(which relates to the first guess but slightly differs in terms of size/intensity)
because now he looked bad, after i shared our private conflict with an outside person who was a mutual friend of ours (the book-reading friend, this is in portland)
and it's not polite to spread problems through the world, that's well poisoning
it's not always to my advantage that i can't lie or keep a secret

well poisoning, as is common, has a latin phrase: ad hominem
 "to the person," attacking the person instead of their point
("ignoratio elenchi" variation) (missing the point)
the worst is when you call out a person's feet of clay, which is their weakness or character flaw, related to a bible story about an otherwise-wonderful statue whose
clay feet caused it to fall to the ground

so, yeah, couple possible issues of mine, and also those facts from looking up well
poisoning on wikipedia here alone in my living room five years after i was called this
it's a miserable truth to me like this: i clearly didn't know the point in the first place
which is a bummer like this: the guy who called me this took photos of barbie dolls against postcard backdrops and he was a trash culture mutant junkie and i adored him
telling you, my problem was with me, and i've always missed him

a note about kids
(by florianne)

kids are important to me
because each one is different
i know because i was different and mean
to each one of them

but I'm almost middle aged, as if to say I'm dead

The question is, what happens when I'm bored with being alone
And a family enters my thoughts, begging to come out of me?
Not that it ever has
Maybe once, when I wondered about a Japanese baby up for adoption
And there it goes, worrying about how it will all work out
My thoughts are what make me sick, really
And I don't need them
I don't need any of it
There's something to be said about just going with the flow
A passive existence that could be acted on
Not reacted to
But there are impulses
It's what makes us animals, really
It's the stop sign
That makes us human
Bound to rules
And that's where the death comes
These milestones are not mine
They're just road surface marking
Painted red, white, and blue
Only on holidays
Never always
No, that's not for the middle aged
That freedom

My Will

To write, one must live
So in the beginning there was I, but along with time-
That blossomed days and nights- weeks and months- years-
Which now is an eternity of utter confusion
Take facades home
Replace the true identities
Of reality....
"Justice" was blinded - not to see the corruption
Weights were never balanced preciously -
The book cradled within his arm - no doubt in left
My mind, 'twas one of trial of error
A wealth, though not rich
But wealth in spirit and truth
Compressed our family into families of their own,
Which were strengthened, I firmly believe

Home Now

Adult is what I want to be,
Which doesn't involve a roommate, in my POV
Even when single
I'll still have the matching bedside tables, though
In case I find a mate
I'll coordinate the carpet with drapes not from Target
Colorful art in gold frames - oil or acrylic - not sloppy movie
posters, Goddamnit
Plants of many varieties - Fiddle Figs or Rubber Trees
Lamps in all corners - wired for energy-saving lightbulbs
A reading chair for the bedroom, with a matching foot stool
A dining table longer than two feet, table cloth optional
Decorative knobs on cabinets, glass or porcelain
Chandeliers, but we don't need to go into details
Office space, even if just a closet
A space to call mine
A graduation, of sorts
Some kind of Pinterest fabrication
A balcony full of citrus trees and tea lights
A built-in book shelf making rainbows out of book spines
A bathtub deep and grout free
Rose candles
Everything I need to feel safe
Until I sit with my feelings
Uncomfortable
Crying in my reading corner
Sitting alone at the longer dining room table
Disconnecting on the balcony
Cozying into meditation
Showering in the salt of the tub
Finding myself in my space
A place to be with me

i was always home

    you were the ones that strayed away
        still always at home
            still you stay away
                what poison do i retain?
                    i am walking out of your lives to live my own
                        may you sink into your own souls in
                            absolute peace and joy

                                          about friendship

do you want to know what a friend is? it's if you can put yourself in his shoes and try walking with yourself. i confess i've been a failure at it many times. so i can't say too much about myself because my shoes have hurt me many times and i tried very hard with broken shoe strings and i remember when there were none. that's why my friends are very special to me. i may have you, but then again, i may have none. parting ways are many.

memo to daughter #4

the man who is completely satisfied with life is already dead
learn the basics of life
before living it

well ok i guess

first of all i didn't even realize there were crickets in my neighborhood
until she pointed at one in my bedroom. then during the night i heard
chirps outside my open windows, clear evidence of a population
but i hadn't realized until told
by the (artistic) girl (who could feel ghosts in rooms)

earlier that night on hollywood hills overlooking the valley we'd kissed
having driven past her college in front of which i meet her one afternoon
to walk the stars toward veggie grill while noticing things we like about the city and each other. she explains hawaiian language to me, calls it pigeon talk, shows me a youtube video

later she shows me a video of her hula dancing
the first time we went out together i met her on my first samuel french theatre & film bookshop visit, where in a reading room
(after actors had concluded their meeting) i sit across from her and take her photo and
instagram her photo with the caption:
material for a chapter in a book about how the world isn't so bad

i like how the world feels with her
her first time at the new beverly cinema was seeing *chungking express*
with me. after the movie, before she rode her fixie home
we circled the sidewalk together in the dark night, with
emotional and cosmic and la-di-dah type electricity between us, each of us smiling

fantastic
i think she's great, she cracks me up, with her i'm in a movie i want to watch
i tell her that while driving her home on the night she asks me to stop driving her home
since what feels great can't last forever, something like that
her heart belongs to another guy elsewhere
she turns 22 and graduates from college later in the year
which i know since we remain facebook friends
i hope she kicks ass as an artist

there's an urgency to move because the rent is too high, which makes me dream about other places, so i go

1
adelaide, australia

staying with my childhood friend who lives on a block of vintage stores with boutique charm
i got a dress made in Japan,
with a Brazilian print
the half whites weren't that special
the beaches were lonely
i didn't even wear a swimsuit
people treat the aboriginals like strangers
it makes me sick
thank god i got to cuddle a koala
took selfies with a kangaroo
they both had a lot of attitude
and yes, i ate kangaroo before i
met one
(sorry)
it was good

2
kona, hawaii

a yoga retreat of menopausal women
searching for happiness
escaping the death of their children
in a jungle of tents
i ate a lot of fruit and garlic cloves
in the midst of my flu
i wrestled with the lava rocks between my toes
slept in a treehouse
determined that vegan icecream was the best, only here

3
joshua tree

more like mars
trees shaped like aliens
rocks stacked, perfectly round
the stars brighter, the sky darker
land stretching out to nothingness
hot for days
i turned 30 here

4
detroit, michigan

i should probably go there
get a new start
in a community getting its own
artists gentrifying condemned houses
which feels wrong, entitled, selfish
but the excuse is
it has potential, like me

5
liechtenstein

the toilet seat talks
and has a rotating mechanical
cleansing unit

6
tamale, ghana

living with the paramount chief
allows me to have my own room
a small foam pad mattress on a concrete floor
the food is the luxury
pounded fufu
mango
rice
beans
avocados, the sweet kind
i sit at a trial between an adulterer and the man he betrayed
(the resolution is a live chicken)
when they celebrate my chief's birthday
drums play
songs are sung
then we pray

7
salem, massachusetts

the town of witches, mostly tourists
used car salesmen
safehouses, AA meetings
you really want to know where my father came from?
go to the casino in Connecticut

8
bracknell, england

my first exposure to countryside
cow poo
attics
tiny staircases
snoopy the dog was pregnant
milk came out of her nipples
daniel painted dungeons and dragons figurines
i loved him
we went to an indoor waterpark
wore floaties
i thought there was no place better on earth
then i got an enya CD
and found god
in my morning dance workout

9
paris, france

all i remember is
my first dick sighting
a homeless man
peeing
on the sidewalk
the synagogues were
the only appropriate
part of that city
and i didn't even pray in
any of them

10
switzerland

lots of pine trees
a mountain of snow
but the best part was
the chocolate icecream that came in a dish
shaped like a whale

11
lake como, italy

if i were to ever
get married
it would
have to be here
if the lake
is still as
warm
as i remember it

12
tel aviv, israel

i had my bat mitzvah
on top of the masada
a holy place
later visited with my college friends
where i found myself being
inappropriately flirtatious
with multiple bad choices
this is now where my first obsession lives
he is getting married next week

13
el capitan, santa barbara

the tiny houses here
make me want to nestle in the forest
give up the city for the simple life
cook food by the campfire every night
with miniature horses and ostriches,
where the pace feels gentle
more serene to my bones

14
big sur

even in the fog,
the bluejays come out
adirondacks sit in the stream
nailed to the cabin wall
is a cheesy waterfall
of bright colors
we talk about how we want it
for our bedroom
we talk about how it's only natural

15
i'm trying to remember all the places i've been, not because i want to impress you, but because it is a good mental exercise

escaping home in places
makes me miss home more
but what is home, really?

ever race against time?
(by florianne)

before you depart
i'm trying
i'm trying
i'm trying
my very best

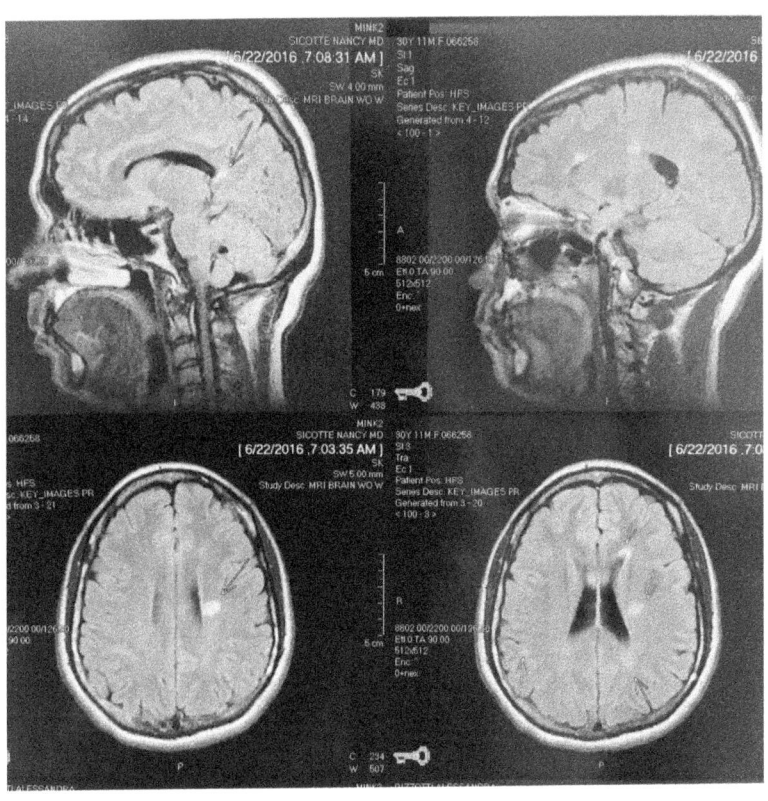

Grief is a Process
  Growth is a Problem

Alessandra Rizzotti
  Shawn Sullivan

Grief is a Process

A division
A Multiplication
A Plus—
    And a minus
Accommodate your grief

According to psychoanalyst Elisabeth Kübler-Ross' 1969 book "On Death and Dying," there are five stages of grief:

> Denial: upon realizing we have lost, we isolate, as if to say it never happened
> Anger: we resent those gone and those who remind us of what we lost
> Bargaining: we want control over reality we can't change, and thus make new realities that somehow mask what no longer is
> Depression: we lose the ability to find a sense of hope and sink deeply into the loss, wanting to be embraced—feeling a sadness akin to confusion
> Acceptance: we allow ourselves to feel what we haven't, then embrace it all as part of who we are or what we will become

Growth is a Problem

as Wikipedia mentions, the psychologist C. D. Ryff cracked open Aristotelian ideals of hedonic well-being, eudaimonia, composing a six-parter:

> one. autonomy
> confidence in opinions
> two. personal growth
> an experienced worldview
> three. self-acceptance
> a comfortable personality
> four. purpose in life
> discovering intention
> five. environmental mastery
> manifesting intention
> six. positive relations with others
> giving to the world as the world gives

Chapter One: Dad is Gone

Denial of a Death

They said the body was decaying
It hadn't yet mushroomed into a tree
The skin passed through the bones
Like the silk of a flag
Gracing the air—
Freedom laid there for weeks
Heavy
Thanksgiving was the last time
We'd love each other out loud
Cross country
When we hugged,
Our fingers touched
The last connection
Now just a vibration
Voices tingling
Through the smalls of our backs

Anger Our Meeting Was Cut Short

We just met, found commonalities
In total, we had 11 years together, 7 of which were blurry mysteries
The 4 years in which we reconnected outweighed the disappearance of 19
Numbers upon numbers
Counted like tacks on a growth chart or bookie sheet
The calls went like this
"Alessandra- It's daddy. What's going on?"
"I dunno."
"What do you not know yet? What the mind can conceive, the mind can achieve."
"It's the feelings I can't place….a sort of an unidentifiable lull."
Blankness passing through telephone wires
"I worry about you."
"Don't. I worry enough."
"Your health is your wealth, so your worry isn't worthy."
Health was never his wealth
Love was what held us up

Bargaining as His Next of Kin

He had land
160 acres in Arizona
No access to water or roads
Sitting on the border of a Navajo reservation
He said it would be the perfect place
For a casino
Or cattle
With no plans for either
20 years, taxes unpaid
His name still sitting on the deed
"I'll seize it from foreclosure," I told the lawyer
"It may not be worth my time or yours"
The truth was, it wasn't even ours in the first place
But his ashes
Must be scattered there
The sun was where he wanted to be

Depression Connects Me

The pain in my chest passed through me like sonic waves
My body telling me more than my feelings were
I couldn't call him anymore
To tell him I was finally doing something important with my life
I wanted to ask him what he was eating for dinner
The void felt heavy
"Loneliness is worse than being alone," he had said
I reached for my phone tree of friends
Little stars that connected my multiple universes
In dial tones
I filled the emptiness temporarily by asking them
To listen
"When will the darkness go away?" I asked
"Never...you need it," they said
And with that, I cupped all the light I had left
Casting it off like a fishing line hooked onto hope
Wishing the sadness would be solved eventually, like a Rubik's cube
I let it sit
Until it criss-crossed, then clicked

Acceptance Dad is Gone for Good

It had been three months since I cleaned my apartment
The boxes of his stuff sat in my doorway, dusty
Waiting to be peeled through like onions
I suspect the fume-like smell that wafted into my bedroom
May have been from his belongings
I blamed the landlord
Accused him of secretly using pesticides to kill an ant hill below me
But it was mold sitting in the cardboard of what he left me
I threw away what I didn't need anymore
I threw away what memories may have existed
I wanted to be held
I wanted someone else to deal with it
It was time to take care of myself
I doused my floors in lavender cleanser
Massaged my body in rose oil
Did breathing exercises and chanted oms
Each bite of food became more mindful
My heart opened and closed, like saloon doors
I got hit
Each time, I felt relief

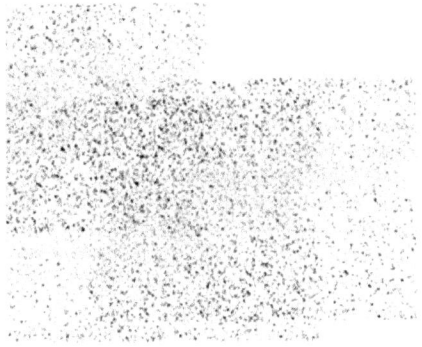

autonomy

autonomy first flourished inside me
during my basic teen years
assisted by my repulsion from the adult world
plus assisted by punk rock and horror movies

perspectives from the underground, the outsiders
sideshows of the malcontent, adore 'em
those who live how they live for as long as they live
being stuck in the battle of life but never stopping their fight
never surrendering to that in this world which wants to drag one down

celebrating not who one isn't but who one is
being in charge of oneself and loud about it
this lights me up
it should be a universal right, you ask me
and here is maybe the only element from this list where i feel comfortable already
which in fact enables me to even speak of eudaimonia
as if it's some topic familiar and known to me

autonomy exercised within a social engagement
a.k.a two people with different reasons for being themselves

so: one person feeling bad sits across from one person feeling good
yeah, for sure: immense emotional distance between their personal feelings

each thinks this about the other: welp, you don't see the same world i do
how can i take you from your world into mine?

emotionally-speaking they exist on separate planets even while together
the person feeling bad mentions to the person feeling good:

all of everything including this moment illuminates the world's badness
and the person feeling good replies fuck the world, i like being with you

do you? is asked, yes! is replied, and what is believed, what is real
and what does it mean that the reality of the table comes from them both

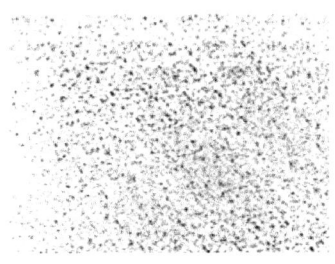

Chapter Two: Parts of My Brain Go Missing

Denial I Have Multiple Sclerosis

It started as migraines
The kind that put me to sleep in face masks and earplugs
Lighting my muscles on fire
Brain lesions popped up
Like little funeral Evites
Pervasive
Inbox annihilators
Consistent reminders
Blips
When my arm went numb
Denial came on like Clerks 2's end credits...endless
Everyone said I was "okay"
My father didn't seem to think his Parkinson's had anything to do with it
My partner blamed it on my period
My mother prepared for someone else to inherit her estate
My brother looked up at-home nurses
Then my legs collapsed
"Don't worry...I'll take you out," I told the dog
A cane was the only thing that held my pride up

Anger It Happened Right Before I Turned 30

"No one will want me this way."
Mobility in my legs gone from time to time
Loud noises deafening serenity
I become so unfocused
My brain wants to escape me
The disassociation is akin to ghosts rising above my body in the afterlife
I'm angry about the lack of
Control—which doesn't exist in any world anyways
The anxiety heightens
I dig fingernails into pillows
Clench blankets
Unable to leave my safety net—
A spiderweb so intricate and structured,
Ready to break at any moment
"I'm ready, God, take me."
My hand jives to
Silence in the air

Bargaining With Human Resources For Peace and Quiet

I asked to work from home so that I could focus
They said it was fine, until it wasn't
Unplanned meetings came up, throwing me off
I preferred the company of the dog, occasional mariachi music, and FedEx drop-offs
Office chatter trapped me
I had yet to make friends,
But was so willing to explain my disease to everyone
Oversharing was my thing
And then someone told me not to mention my disability
Because it would
Hinder chances of
Staying employed
Being loved
Living
I refused to be inauthentic
Fear couldn't get me down

Depression Soothed by Otherness

All the grief was stored in my arthritic hand and lower back
It bubbled up to my chest
Taking homeopathic medicines kept me going
I sat on the couch to watch 'X Files'
Reveling in the possibility that life on other planets
Could be better than this

Acceptance This Is My New Body

The last time
I got intimate
With another body,
My leg went numb
I had no idea
That lack of feeling
Would happen again,
With more frequency
When they took out
The accordion file
Of my medical records
Displaying the brain scans
It felt like
I was at a flea market
Looking at oddities
I'd never buy
The progression of splotches
Around my frontal lobe
Geotargeted an explanation
For all my emotional outbursts
Things started making sense
People came forward
To show support
As if I was dying
And sure, that was happening
But a new person emerged
She was better
She was stronger
She had a positive outlook
She was going to be okay

personal growth

a fundamental fear within personal growth
is in regard to whether one is growing into the kind of person one wants to be
or should be or could be or
if one even wants to be a person(!)

with autonomy and without personal growth one feels as if in total control of a whole bunch of bullshit sometimes, maybe often or never, depends
 i can feel like that when looking into the mirror (which i might confuse as the world)

seeing another person on the street see me
can cause me to wonder/worry
how i appear when looked at by another
i often desire to look and be seen different than how i am
and i often suspect other people as meanies so i don't want to be like them either

this problem becomes a philosophical cul-de-sac within my curious existentialism
i am ready for new experience, new potential, but i seem to be arriving at nothing

every night going to bed i think may i not be myself tomorrow... but of course i'm always myself and, thing is, who am i and who should i be?

oh i keep going
and
personal growth problems can overwhelm professional growth successes in sour ways
same with romance

some tough decisions have to be made regarding me being in total control of my identity
and which kind of human i'll be in this world i share with others
 but oh, i can't tell, and oh, there are a lot of them
other humans and tough decisions to make while becoming oneself
the enormity of it all can be overbearing to me
since i can't figure out
the person i'll like being

will i ever see myself as a person i want to be?(?)

worldly data collected as personal growth while visiting the LA Art Book Fair

"if i had something to do with the making of time."

things i don't know the totality of, experienced through pure observation

sidestory: a trip into little tokyo, up [street], a crowd
of people i'm the only white person i
see until i pass two white women holding
hands. this moment of life i cherish because it reminds me of textures outside my
own. textures that live around me and away from me. a store: pop tokyo the village center. later we eat here in a cross-cultural diner that has hamburgers burritos sushi and chow mein
i order a burger that tastes cooked from a freezer

name of an art company (imagining): petzel

a favorite: t-shirt of a dog with a smile, tongue dangling
wearing purple-rimmed sunglasses which reflect a palm tree sunset
"los angeles" written in pink cursive below this portrait

dead wrestlers
dead wrestler ii
chapbooks with earthy-brown fibrous covers featuring circular icons

colors on the table, colors in the crowd

i hear screeching from a guitar while i write this poem alone but with others at a
picnic table outside the museum
mostly screeching guitar sometimes bursts of "everybody
talking, everybody talking"

and these details mean i should
vacation
launch a vessel outside my normal

write and remind myself of my hunger as an artist for art

colour code
valley cruise
their pinks and purples!

all the types of people and the ways arts share people's shapes

now at: the "go for broke" monument outside the museum
where morgan kailyn and i visit to smoke cigarettes and pot

away from other people, not wanting our smoke to bother others we stand in the sun, i search for shadows
which i see in the stone columns of a nearby monument
moving to stand there instead, alone but with others

this writing being a dimension of my personal growth

attempting to float toward and away from being only myself, i find help: Alessandra!
plus
Maggie Nelson reminds me:
a studied evasiveness has its own limitations
its own ways of inhibiting certain forms of happiness and pleasure

that is to say (i'm saying:) i crave not the life nor the philosophy of the loner rebel-outsider
since that sounds to me full of self-imposed boundaries

staying open 24/7 is my goal

thinking: any rebel who sounds like a rebel has limited rebellion

my desire is to sound unlimited

which i've figured out best (only?) through emotions
remembering: Oscar Wilde wrote that people's emotions are more delightful than their ideas

projecting particulars from my thoughts and heart onto this page
this book has more of a formal plan than my life

creating this book with Alessandra
from that which dwells in us
bliss

other people help me
to quote Nelson again, she makes a vibrant diss on Freud
which type of diss i always adore hearing from intellectuals
she describes his career full of theoretical concepts that willfully annihilate nuance and, i'll mention it:
my theoretical concepts annihilate my nuances when i'm alone

i long to look beyond my own hands (how well do i describe my hands, wondering)
and struggling at finding where to look
i look at Alessandra and she helps
this book does, there are her hands too

Chapter Three: I Become Single

Denial The Relationship is Over

I got a temporary studio apartment in Koreatown
Because the separation would be a phase
Then he moved a girl and her pomeranian into our old place
It was beyond done
It was done because I said so,
But I didn't want a replacement
How could I be replaced?
He turned over my keepsakes
In an oversized box labeled "Miscellaneous"
Put the rest in a storage unit and said I could go when I was ready
It was a nice boundary
Then he expected a hug,
Which crossed the fence we were creating
Saying 'no' was the best connection I had to myself
The only tie I wanted to hold onto was the fact he knew my father
He'd be the only lover who ever did

Anger from Comparing and Despairing

I'm living in a shitty apartment for a higher rent than he pays for our old two bedroom
It's when the plants are cut down at my new place that I lose faith things will get better
His new girlfriend adopts my old friends, and I let them go
I starve myself when I can't go to the same burrito place anymore
My dog feels the resentment
I see it in her eyes
It's as if she thinks she's guilty
I assure her she's the best thing that's happened to me

Bargaining For My Things Back

I wanted to possess what little I had left
Including my broken mug still sitting in our (his) kitchen cabinet
The oven mits
The coat hangers
The paint brushes
I asked for them in an email
"You're crazy," he said
I wish it hadn't been true

Depression From Finding Myself

It's time to
Climb outside my skin
Get a new balcony for my thoughts
His new lady has a ring around her finger
Heart-shaped
It holds all my grief —
The person I wanted to be but never became
The positivity I never let myself see
The gratitude I never expressed —
I slip through my pillow
Disappear for a while, then wake up heavy
Like a wet towel
It's time to be worthy of love
I must find why I am worthy

Acceptance I'm Alone And It's Wonderful

In solitary confinement
I find a community that shows me what self-love looks like
It is intimate—
Groups of women
Crying to each other about the things that make them feel
Less-than
It's like a coven
Connecting to something bigger than myself
I search again for what I like to do, be, eat, breathe
Lavender, jasmine, crystal, sage
Meditating, making eggs, stretching in the morning
Beekeeping in afternoons
Being alone at night
I become
Ready to share myself as is

self-acceptance

oof
what then can i say from beyond personal growth?
mustn't i be there in order to know...

but, well, eh, autonomy was mentioned first

sooooooo
i'll mention i'm picturing:
a direct link between results from one's personal growth and self-acceptance
the words this is who i am, i'm worth being alive
fly like doves from my tongue

yeah, pretty sure, self-acceptance can be a culmination of personal growth
but also
self-acceptance is helpful for personal growth
and, reminder
the only thing i know is i'm the one who's in control of myself
in addition to being imperfect by nature and design

i.e.
my technique
for self-acceptance
comes from myself
and my current mantra is
fake it 'til you make it

what does self-acceptance demand from a person during these
internet days? maybe everything, definitely not nothing, ok i
forget

then
because i'm always me
being me

i'm saying now, for the internet people or readers from
elsewhere
whom i'm currently imagining and who exist:
outside the thoughts
expressed by these poems
lives the person writing
and what does the reader know of me?
should you check my facebook?

please don't, i'm afraid of you
please do, since i'm afraid of being alone

i don't have a point, i have a feeling
always outside my point is my feeling and sometimes inside my
feeling is a fear

the writer of *Diary of an Oxygen Thief* said, in an interview i read
that in the days of social media
being an anonymous writer
allows more imagination for the reader

then i'll mention this
as if from the blue
but, not
from where my feelings have been while writing this poem

here is a quote from *Oxygen*, thanks for reading:

I felt all the cobwebs billow
then blow away in a warm flush of summer air
that seemed to close around me

Chapter Four: I Let Go of Work In Pursuit of Higher Education

Denial I'm Not My Job Title

I used to weigh my self-worth on the scale of a job title
What I was earning was who I was
My father thought quite the opposite
He led a pauper lifestyle
His happiness was built on a state of mind
He said it wouldn't matter what I was doing
As long as I was happy just 'being me'
When the fax machine scanned my ego
It came up blank, then turned into
A hurricane of paperwork
Meant to settle into a sense of accomplishment
Then disburse into nothingness—ink blots of faded hope
Trickling against the edges of a good piece of scratch paper—
The kind for writing notes with—nothing substantial
I held dreams in a folder but never opened it
My business cards were ordered, but never asked for
The title under my name read: 'Good enough'
I printed alternates with: 'Doesn't give a shit'

Anger I Can't Get What I Want

The plan was to go to grad school and work
But when work didn't see my plan in their cards,
I thought about not going to grad school
The decisions I had to make for
Higher education
Seemed unfair
Choices became sacrifices
I had to find a sense of self
Beyond the 9 to 5

Bargaining for a Shift

When the night shift became available, I bargained for a shift in personal needs
It seemed reasonable to want to afford living
But the reality of having an immune disease required sleep
Wants became sidenotes
I scheduled parts of myself like a crew of teammates
Nothing ever lined up perfectly

Depression I Couldn't Have it All

Work structured me
I wrote an email to my team each day
A list of priorities
Hopes
Desires
Most of the time dreams fell by the wayside
The goal was to just get shit done
What was I supposed to do when it was time to stop it all?
I feared becoming lazy
I feared not having the money to eat out and order in
All of this
Was not worth harping on
I couldn't have it all
That would have to be okay

Acceptance The Future Will Live in The Grey

I've been unemployed two times in my life—
This will be the third, though this time was a choice
To have a future
As in, my life with letters behind my name
A graduate degree
Which could lead to opportunity or
Be an epic failure
But
I have an instinct I'll be fine
Whatever way chooses me
Is the way I'll go

purpose in life

frankly,
and this is common to me
not quite sure
i'm achieving my current writing purpose
of conveying an idea to share with others

working on it
i think i drift off track back on track off track et cetera

reminder:
my topic is eudaimonia
which is one's personal sense of wellbeing
and my thoughts are on how this topic might apply to my life experience
(while barely knowing about myself or eudaimonia, barely processing my life experience)

and i like being around people although i'm terrible at it and not even sure i've mentioned that yet

anyway it does seem like you have to put yourself together
before you create action in this world
and action is purpose
i'm working on my social actions and some other ones too

knowing this world isn't made by what i think but by what i do
i have to know what i want to do and do it
which has been this problem of mine, in terms of figuring things out
this relates to aspects of self-acceptance and personal growth
and autonomy alone is not a purpose in life

tripping out on my life's purpose for a poem's length (example)

this serious topic reflects upon my life's course
which appears to exist within a forest
headed toward a place which i can't see

Chapter Five: I Lost My Old Self While Briefly Coupling

[Note to reader: After my five year relationship, I attempted to date again as a new person. The old self had to die off. This is an account of that experience.]

Denial It Was Scary Growing Into Someone New

When I don't want to feel scared
I spend time fantasizing about the future
As you do when you're browsing the aisles of a grocery store
I imagine myself being 'adult' in a societal normal sorta way
Maybe a ring around my finger
Maybe regular dinner parties for friends of the 40+ variety
Maybe investing in real estate
Maybe having an office where I balance taxes
Then the fantasies come crashing down
With the perceived realities of my capabilities
My old self ruminates on past behaviors such as:
Being more concerned about someone else's thoughts than my own feelings
Wanting to be in love for the sake of it
Fearing abandonment
Fearing cohabitation
Fighting for independence outside of a relationship
My old self died off while briefly coupling, causing my new self to fall apart
My old and new pieces could have stayed together, like a refurbished computer
But I didn't want to make it work
New was too scary and scary would have made me grow faster
I had to let the old self float away

Anger From Not Being Angrier

To lose my old self was pretty serious
Truth is,
I wasn't at all angry about that part of coupling with someone
My old self was angrier that I wasn't angered
I let the breakdown of my old self happen naturally like when
Food goes bad sitting in the fridge
It could have happened sooner
But I let myself "be in the moment" more
When I wanted to know all the answers too soon
It made him pull away
The space between us was sacred
But filling it with darkness made it all slip away

Bargaining for Time With Myself

We both agreed that time alone was pretty good to have
Being around each other too often would take its toll
The old self battled against that
She wanted 24/7 attention
The new self marked out time for herself
It would happen weeknights after work,
The times he was still working
But then the new self wanted to fill the void with other people
Friends
Strangers
Coworkers
The new self had to learn how to be alone
She had to let the old self feel pain

Depression From Not Being Comfortable With My New Self

The moments of discomfort between us were the times when silence happened
The old self wanted to fill the void with entertainment and questions about each other
Smiles and giggles—
Cuddles and such
When I hit a lull, I worried I was boring
The insecurity bred self-hate
Six months and I feared the end was happening
I sabotaged the good
I had to remind myself what I was grateful for:
Finding someone who listened
Finding someone who was empathetic
Finding someone who was smart
It would be possible to find it again even when it didn't work out

Acceptance I Can Coexist With Another, Someday

There's beauty in knowing that parts of me will die
Those parts will just grow into another
And that's okay
Very bonsai of me
Someone can love me
And I can love myself
And all of it can happen together
Just like light and dark happen together
Without one, there isn't the other
Without the old, there is no new
Someday, I'll coexist with another
Once I find acceptance within

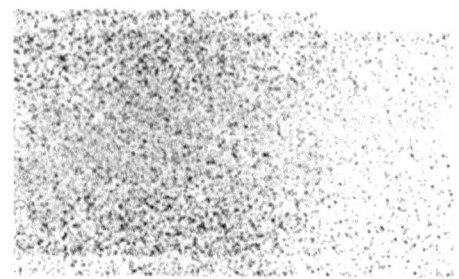

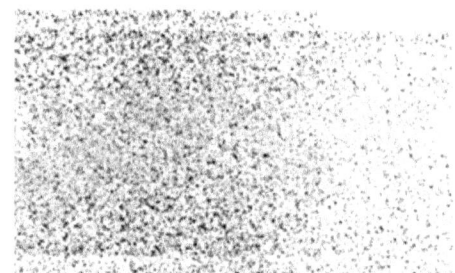

environmental mastery

a thing i know is my superior environmental masteries
are products of my frequent hobby: self-reflection

always when i (always) examine my past i feel i can spot a problem of mine
sometimes, after more examination, i spot other smaller and bigger problems

which means i spot my problems better than i fix them
and it isn't common for me to feel like the master of my living environment, my daily life

i struggle with human complexities
plus all their manifestations which, no, i don't often feel in control of, and only sometimes can vaguely remember

these poems: self-portrait attempts at environmental mastery

considering the reading of these poems
similar to looking at me
i'll confess: i've seen some photos
i have my bad angles

do my poems have bad angles?
by being like me, i don't see how they can't
so i think they do, even while i write
and i think the same about me even while i live

i keep living, keep writing
and later after time reflection and growth i'll wish to edit some poems
but the poems are living as they are here now, written by me, as i am now

Chapter Six: Losing Happiness From Things That Used to Regularly Make Me Happy, As In I Am Depressed and My Therapist is Worried

Denial I'm A Mess

When I broke out in pimples, it was clear
Shit was going down
The birth control must have done it
I felt totally out of control
My stress levels, visible
Aka my hair was no longer getting combed
I disregarded the shower
The spa stopped being a safe-haven
I wanted to battle my therapist in a boxing ring
I ate toast for all meals
Crackers were a treat
I was broken
Her telling me so confirmed all fears of such

Anger I Don't Remember The Last Time I Was Truly Happy

Happiness really comes in cycles, like the washer and dryer
Bleached when necessary
I'd like to sort and fold what gets me down
But I'm just ripping through it all like old towels for dish rags
Slow, painful, to the point of rage
Tangled shreds of fabric just hanging down
When was the last time I was truly happy?
Probably when I knew someone loved me
But I still didn't love myself, so how completely happy could that be, really?
That's a rhetorical question, by the way

Bargaining for The Space To Have Happier Feelings

Listening to sad music helps me hear that I'm not alone
But then I'm wrapped up in fantasy
I bargain between bass and guitar to lighten my mood
But I've been in lower registers forever

Depression from Depression

The ship sank
I thought a narwhal had pierced through the hull
The reality was my heart didn't feel safe
So it dragged me down to the underbelly of the sea
Darkness bred darkness bred darkness

Acceptance I'm Not Letting Go Of My Lows

I'm learning to understand that
What I'm feeling in the moment
Is not permanent
Instead of pushing those feelings down
I must embrace them
I find a level of comfort in knowing
My belief in my unworthiness
Will pass
I want to disappear
But I know my feelings will instead
The lows will let go of me
Once I let go of them

positive relations with others

i'm mad at myself
i'm going to try to be okay with you
if i can pause being mad at myself and divert my efforts
toward being ok with you
(possible
i can feel light with another during my worst)

my worry about the categories within eudaimonia
probably compose a backdrop
of a fight within me while i sit with you
[this described in the second poem about autonomy]

i might become mad at another person
because i'm mad at myself
and what will the other person think then?
this is both common and not helpful:
they'll reflect anger back
let me see how it feels (we both already knew!)

the anger i have which i sometimes stick myself within
i'm going to try to
become better at
unsticking myself
to become calm again
this is
hard to do
after anger has been introduced
like i said it's a very sticky problem

on the topic of
self-acceptance being helpful for arriving at resolutions
i'd like to repeat
my current self-acceptance mantra: *fake it 'til you make it*
i want to remember
most of the time i'm fighting with another person
neither of us want to be fighting

[omitted section that i just created: autonomous by choice,
confused for eternity
working on trying to figure out how this world works
and trying to work on figuring out me within it]

theory vs. practice: reflections: the current status of my eudaimonia

following our quite-late phone conversation, i think around 4am i sleep
then beginning my new day i wake twice
first at 7, when i stroll outside
then i sleep again then i wake again at 10, call then text her at 11
she texts me around 12
i call her, she doesn't pick up
i text her
she texts me about things to consider from our previous night and future
i feel hopeful, excited
love will win, i am sure
thank heaven for love
i call her, she doesn't pick up
i text her some love
she texts me to clarify that we did indeed break up the night before

realizing:
learning the night's lesson she learned about needing to break up with me, fuck

then i call her again, then again she doesn't pick up

it's afternoon and the sun peeks through my blue-curtain's edges and my room is quiet
except within my body my feelings are strident sirens warning of approaching despair
i text her approximately something about that
texts which sound like me anyway, and relating to how awful this feels

we make plans for her to return my apartment keys to my mailbox

i figure i know when she'll return my keys
that's when she does
she leaves my keys with a note in cursive green ink
I am beyond sorry that I've hurt you. I love you

in that moment i have a lot of trouble understanding/believing the I love you part
i walk outside, see her across the street, run to her

she tells me things have been getting worse between us
and my love-filled eyes cannot see what she means
knowing there was a problem last night, still
honestly not yet seeing between us our problem bigger than our love
and within me

we both have fears she says
i mention *this, what's happening, is actually my fear*

what is your fear? i ask
she reminds me *i've told you*
which problem of mine is she thinking of i wonder, asking
please, tell me the fear
she doesn't say anything

i look her in her sunglasses and ask if our love is one she believes in
she shakes her head no
thank God there's more than belief, but oh that headshake hurts
she shakes her head a normal amount
but i'd like to repeat that she does
i mention *last night on the phone you said you want to be with me, and today you don't?*
she shakes her head yes
she shakes her head a normal amount, then i turn and run from her

i can't believe it
and upon immediate reflection i really can't believe it

almost back to my apartment
i then run back down Fairfax toward her
she's across the street on a sun-kissed sidewalk

she smokes a cigarette now
i ask her *i'm sorry but i really can't believe it, what changed between last night and today?*
what did i do?

she says *you didn't do anything*
it's me, i need to think about me

i ask *did i make your days worse?*
she doesn't say anything, her face emotionless, except with kind of a small smile in my opinion
as if maybe she could not say i had made her days worse

i ask her if she'll take off her sunglasses
so i can look into her eyes

what does it feel like to look into the eyes of the person who
told you yesterday that she wants to be with you and
today stands away from you with firm assurance?

my emotions are falling down a chasm the walls of which i cannot clutch
and i want to cry but i can't because all i am now is confusion and terror
i tell her, looking into her (beautiful) eyes
you, all of you, you're everything i want in a person

she doesn't say anything

i ask *can i learn from this mistake... is there no option but us ending... can i learn?*

she doesn't say anything
so this will be how i learn, how i always learn

i ask *is there anything else you want to say to me, is this it?*
she says *i've said all i need to*

after she's put back on her sunglasses i tell her
i don't know what's going on but i'm absolutely sure this isn't love
because being broken up never feels like love at the time, nah

i still can't realize what i'd done to myself the night before
during mistakes which i know i'd made
but which i'm learning were supernatural
all i can realize is what i can see now, this wasteland of emotions i'm in
i say something like *this is the saddest day i've ever had*
i feel my bottom lip quiver and
i turn around, feeling that statement and my trembling lip the only
current points i have to make

while walking back i send her my clarifying texts:
Brutal
And
Far worse than i ever imagined, if that brings you joy

my actions and thoughts becoming a messy spiral which i'm losing her
and myself within

then walking back to my apartment i see
Morgan getting out of Kailyn's car
arriving for our hangout we'd planned

inside my apartment we smoke pot
i tell him the story of our breakup, from both sides, mainly from the
perspective of what i did wrong
immediately sensing my today is a result of my own blunderings
but there is a love in my head which blocks my total view
and through time my thoughts process
memories of a faded romance
this afternoon while the sun licks Morgan's neck and face
while he sits on the green cloth chair against the window
he tells me *i like your window view*

Morgan is a good friend, listens to me tell him things
i purge my emotions after my breakup, a very human quality
then Morgan shows me the proof of his book
Stuck in an Elevator Between the 12th & 14th Floors of an Apartment Building on Rossmore

and we chat about *The Stages,* and we chat about *Violent Letters*
and Bukowski's letter
making plans and dreams for Neon Burrito Publishing

then outside we smoke cigarettes
(this while i have strep throat a.k.a. tonsilitis)

so through time, reflection and during conversations with Morgan
my relationship blunders become visible in my thoughts
 as monsters which crawl out from my darkness

i'm always such a champ at gaining personal knowledge
by making mistakes
i seem only to learn from mistakes
and i sure am in a situation where all i can do is learn

a bit later i text her
No, of course it doesn't bring you joy
and others realizations i'm having
including that i know she's not meaning to hurt me and i know
she never did

then i'm inside New Beverly Cinema
watching *Hi Diddle Diddle* with Morgan
it's a good one, although i don't fully watch it
at one point i legit think *i'd rather be dead than live through this night
and through more days like this*
and i think more about the errors i made to bring myself here
and then within my reflections i don't discover monsters of her darkness
which makes me realize how i'd invented through my fears our monsters
Quentin Tarantino sits in front of Morgan and me during *Hi Diddle Diddle*
that's cool, since i like how much QT likes movies
this being his theater and a movie he picked, his print
i watch *Hi Diddle Diddle* while having self-reflections
this a solid movie night

after the first movie and before the second
Morgan and i stroll around the block, me telling him some of the
reflections i've been having
i tell him she'd mentioned angry, defensive, selfish and
emotionally manipulative behaviors coming from me
now i can see what she meant

i send her another text while on the lobby steps as *The Bachelor's
Daughters* begins inside
i text her that i'd said she couldn't see from my eyes, recognizing that i
hadn't seen from hers

i'm beginning to see more clearly what happened in our past
whom i'd transformed myself into

oh i didn't like the person i'd been either, looking at him with her eyes

during *The Bachelor's Daughters* Morgan and i are behind QT again
nice
at one point the film burns in the projector
Morgan and i go outside to smoke while repairs are made
then we return to *The Bachelor's Daughters* which continues
and which i leave from for a minute after
my phone buzzes multiple times and a call arrives
of course the buzzing makes me wonder/hope
it's my mother
i text her that i'm in a movie
she texts about wanting to visit for breakfast tomorrow
(because i've recently told my sister about some unrelated-to-this-story worries i've been having)
i text her *i'm fine, stories you've heard have been exaggerated*
then i return to finish *The Bachelor's Daughters*

after the movie
my mother convinces me to have breakfast with her tomorrow

then Morgan and i return to my place
we chat some more
he helps ground me in my situation's reality
he helps me think from outside my current gloom
he doesn't know her he's only met her
but i think he speaks of humans well
he helps grow within me the perspective she'd mentioned
that this is a decision she's made not against me but for herself

then Morgan leaves, around the normal time she leaves from work
having known how she'd drop off my keys
i'd also guessed where her car is
i check: her car is still parked
i know when she gets off work at night
she prefers someone to walk her back to her car
(her work is by where i live, and also i work where she does)
it's a friendly gesture to walk her to her car this night...
this is how i gesture:
i walk from her car to the street, then back to her car
is she right here? I wonder while spinning my head and walking

i wonder about time and if i should be doing this
i'm feeling risky, there's the possibility of her not wanting to see me
figuring though that i'd rather see her than not see her
and i don't feel angry or critical
i wait outside her work until the latest guessable time for her departure
i even stand until a little later, where i always stand (but a little further, because of nervousness)

through paranoia i think she's already seen me anyway
and i text her confessing
i'd gone to walk her to her car but hadn't found her
i return to my apartment alone
buying water and cigarettes along the way

then while carrying water and smoking a cigarette on my street corner
(where i've stopped to look and see her car still parked)
a car stops in front of me and i hear my name
then i look and see a mutual coworker of ours driving
in his passenger seat another mutual coworker
i notice them in total silence, they laugh-smile
then i notice her in the back of his car
i can't see her face, i see her shirt
did she smile too? what's my guess?
his car takes off, heads down the street
i stand there a moment, think again that i'd like to see her
i walk down the street toward her car
i see her get dropped off and enter her car
when i'm a half-block away her headlights flip on and
she turns down the first street, away from me
smoked, i think, sure she saw me, so i call her
leave her a message mentioning this situation
telling her i won't hold it against her but i can't believe it
then i text her that i really won't hold it against her, considering the day
then she calls me
tells me she hadn't seen me in the street
mentions she'd mentioned to our coworkers in the car me on the corner
i ask her if she's being honest about not seeing me in the middle of the street running toward her car
with my raised and waving hands
she says of course she's being honest
i agree we don't have trust issues and she must be being honest
we share feelings of laughter about that and about the day a little
for example: regarding a waitress at my breakfast place, Swingers
where she's gone with me
the waitress who asks about her now
i ask if i can tell the waitress she died in a tragic ship accident out at sea
she tells me i can
i ask her to tell me a story from her day and she does
oh her stories, how much i like them!, another topic related to me liking everything about this woman
i mention a regret of mine is in our two months together we hadn't taken one photo of us
we speak of friendship between us now
she seems worried about the prospect of us being friends
but promises she'll see *The BFG* with me
there's some silence too, things like that
and i have pure happiness from being on the phone with her
i ask her if she brought up our breakup at work,

she begins to tell me how she did a bit
then she says the day felt gloomy and suddenly says *i have to go*
i think-say *okay*
i feel lucky that she called, that had been sweet of her in my opinion
after our conversation i feel light because of how we can still communicate

the next morning i wake and i don't feel light at all
my feelings guiding me (always), i text her
that i hadn't expected
all of sorrow's weight to pin me against my bed today
text something like that, reminding her that she'd been my everything
these texts after when in the last text i'd said i wouldn't text her about us anymore

then i meet my mother, who i discover is with my sister
for breakfast at Canter's
neither my mother nor sister know anything
about my last day or its context
i'm glad to be around family
i ask about other family members

my sad thoughts make me sometimes feel so small
cause my worries to feel so huge
and hearing the lives of others brings dimensions, perspectives back into my sense of this world

after we eat mother goes to the bathroom before we leave
and i begin mentioning to my sister how proud i am of our mother
while telling her this, to my surprise, my eyes feel prepared for tears
so i take some speaking breaks and talk slowly
i say *her strength inspires me*
then i want to tell my sister
how much it means to me that they came today
except more speaking breaks occur, to avoid those tears
then after my sister says *i'm glad you're appreciating mom*
i tell her *about to include you too*
but then we notice mother leaving the bathroom and we head out
i not having told my sister what i wanted to tell her
how much she means to me

i return to my apartment feeling stronger
feeling reminded there is a world outside my worries
sometimes on occasion often and never my feelings are to me all of what's true
but what about my next feeling, will it be the same and/or different?
and at best i'm my own tiny truth in a big world

i think i have work at 4
work calls to tell me i don't have to work today because of my tonsillitis

under the sun i walk to work to ask about sick pay
and because i want to buy some books i'd ordered
so i go to work, ask about sick pay, buy Fante's *Full of Life* and Bukowski's *Bring Me Your Love*
i see her working at a cash register but i go to another register on another floor
avoiding her, guessing she wouldn't want to see me

i begin working on this book i'm glad to be making with Alessandra
she gets me, i get her, philosophically
we ride horses together through the forest of poetry and life
hours pass as i work on other poems

then while outside strolling i begin to think of her
our relationship clearly over, i chainsmoke, hours pass
me thinking about a voicemail i'd like to leave her on the topic of this being my bad
how can i make the message not about me, what is the message for her? i wonder
i determine to tell her it was my own fears which became our reality
the monsters we had had come from me
but phrase it differently
i compose some drafts for this message on my phone's Voice Memos
until making drafts feels to drift me away from the intentions i'd like my voicemail to represent
the honesty in voice and words
the heart... i always hope to preserve mine as much as i can whenever i can whatever it is
and upon review of our relationship my conclusion is she understands love better than i do
it was foolish of me to ever think or say she didn't/doesn't
and my words are not always truth, sometimes they're my fears or something else
i don't like the sound of myself sometimes either
i sometimes make bad sounds within reality

it's after sunset on july 4 and fireworks have started
and after lonely-walking in my neighborhood for hours, i leave my apology voicemail for my recent ex-gf
focusing on telling her that it was only me who brought us down
since i don't want her to ever feel guilt or anything like that when she thinks of us
i mention i was our destructive force
the realization of which doesn't allow me to undo my destruction
but allows me to leave her this message

then i eat dinner at Benito's and feel regret about leaving the message
the spiral i'm in which i'm now seeing, i send her a clarification text
a text regarding my voicemail, which i mention had been my attempt at an amends

(in the text i write amend, me always somehow exposing an
imperfection or two)
i tell her i hope my voicemail reached its intention of saying
she wasn't our problem, i was our problem

then i send an apology text for it being July 4, ask her to
hold that fact against the calendar
and this is what i sometimes do when reflecting upon a spiral:
create a new spiral
this one outside the last but now its own crisis

i want to read/and/or/definitely write a book titled *How to let go*

i go home, take a 500mg Cephalexin, work on some other poems
then finally i write this poem

now, this poem completed, what do i see?
how much i think of myself
all this work it takes me to see myself
i hope to begin seeing myself as another person

analytical self-analysis of mine searches for and does expose to me
many flaws i have, some of which i believe she accurately described as
self-serving emotional manipulation
she was accurate from the perspective of me sometimes sounding
as if i believe in my worries i shouldn't have

in regard to the final phone call night
how could i tell her how easy it is to love me
while making it seem so difficult?
emotionally cycloptic and myopic in perspective
i didn't know to regret the night while it happened
i know i would have regretted it any next day
but the next day being our breakup day prompted
my thorough examination of our final night
in terms of what i'd done and why and how, writing this poem
and, yup, that which had been getting worse in us was me, and
that night yes i was my worst

i remember her stopping the conversation to throw up once
saying she felt sick
then she called me back, mentioning only once a little later she almost
felt like throwing up again
she tonally criticized *this one-hour conversation* regarding my fears
regarding our day we didn't spend together
how i'd wanted to see her, and i'd kept telling her

i didn't/don't hold this all against her, but so why did i mention it?
we hadn't made plans and this day was for herself... these weren't
matters i disagreed with

but irrational sadness in my thoughts of her created
my sad self-implosion
my emotional meltdown and the annihilation of our relationship

my true worries our final phone night?
the ones outside absurd instances within love addiction?
the whole time i was simply glad to be on the phone with her
talking about anything, not worried at all

but descriptions of internal irrationality sound totally fucking irrational
me being irrational was all of the problem and what occurred
it's never helpful to share with another person an irrational fear you're having about them
explaining some fears makes it sound as if explaining the person's problems

it's as if i'd been telling her
my eyes are insane now, please look through them instead
since my view had not been better

irrationality often comes from an emotional bird which flies by me
and which i jump upon, and its wings i sometimes curl my legs upon
hoping i'll fly toward my dreams which are away from my fears
without realizing i'm flying on a dead bird

for example
i asked for more love from a girl who gave me all the love a person should have
testing limits i broke my limits and broke us

if only that night (classic)
without being told, without our conversation even having happened i could have realized
there was nothing to be upset about, no real problem
it wasn't a night of worries which needed to happen or exist

and i wonder how i can ever love another person so that they know it
so that love shines through my bad moments
which bad moments sometimes concern the topic of love

i had mentioned to her that i'm a paranoiac and a romantic
which means it's logical my meltdown related to her
and that day in my sickness and solitude i missed her not only
way too much but also from a shattered perspective
oh it was a bad day for me in every way, from tonsils to head to heart

she was sometimes so sharp about spotting when i was creating a problem for myself
but in the end she became sick of hearing about my imaginary worries
which included her

i'll miss when certain times she'd just tell me, for example
perhaps with a laugh
you're being ridiculous
and smile
and i'd remember how much she loves me, gets me

once while i kissed her in her car i asked her
do you want to finish your cigarette first?
the question related to matters of using her lips
she then turned and flicked her cigarette out the window
turned to me and put her hands around my face, pulled me in and
kissed me, made my emotions shake

from the Benito's parking lot to picking me up under the marquee
to Zuma Beach to my heart
instead of the book of poems about loving her i'd wanted to write
there's this
these reflections which don't change me as a person
since i see the problem, think that night shouldn't and couldn't have
been created
there's the lesson and there's the mistake
there's air and tomorrow and that's it

reading the title of this poem, which poem in fact doesn't exist, creates a symbol of readerly power, according to the writer, who thinks he's being a bit sneaky with this little whatever he's doing but, it's for you the reader indeed, thanks for reading, here's a Chasidic saying from the 18th century

just as the hand, held before the eye, can hide the tallest mountain
so the routine of everyday life can keep us from seeing the vast radiance
and the secret wonders
that fill the world

Afterword: Grief is a Loss of Connection To Myself, Which Just Means I Must Find Acceptance Within

I grieve sometimes before I know I've lost someone
I do it to prepare
It's an act of guarding myself
Against more pain
I learned early on that if I believed a person didn't exist,
I could detach from them altogether
And never worry again
If I grieve now, I
Won't feel it as hard later
If I know what's coming,
I'll accept it later
Upon grieving deep-seated feelings
From the past,
I become absent
Which is a disservice
To who I am
And whom others in my life might become

Chapter One: My Father
I didn't know him
I pined for what I thought he was
When he died, I created a fantasy of where he wanted to go
I buried the first set of ashes beside his father
The sun shined above us as snow surrounded us
Soldiers folded a flag in honor of his service
A horn played
We toasted him with Coca-Cola
Read cryptoquotes he solved —
Ate pasta putunesca
Drank wine glasses full of memories
The second set of ashes were taken to the desert
160 acres in Arizona picked him up in a storm
A rainbow appeared
Beetles guided me to a piece of driftwood shaped like a triangle, a circle piercing through Foreverness wrapped in a soothing symbol of recovery

Chapter Two: My Multiple Sclerosis
Something unexpected can either bring misery or strength
In my case, resiliency
There's self-pity to be had only for small moments
What others think of me is not my business
I can only show them that I am capable and worthy
I am a new person and it is wonderful
If anything, I grieve for those who can't see that

Chapter Three: My Five-Year Relationship
There's something so heartbreaking about not knowing who someone is
After spending each day together
The lack of intimacy made things harder
Our minds never met on the same level
We loved on the surface, but not on the inside
The home we built was full of fantasy — what could be versus reality
Delusions upon delusions upon delusions
Distance
Coupled with tension
I fought for what wasn't
It's a relief we didn't hold onto each other
I grieve what I missed out on, but there was so much I learned that there was nothing to really miss
I grew from the absence
I grew from the break
The emptiness from the loss filled me later

Chapter Four: Unemployment
Identity can be wrapped up in so many things— where we come from, whom we love
But for some reason we put so much importance on what we do
I certainly still do
The legacy I want to leave is the future I want to create
I grieve the lack of self-confidence that made me delay pursuing my dreams
But now's the time to change that story
And that's okay

Chapter Five: A Brief Stint in Dating
It's uncomfortable and strange to see myself grow alongside a new person
To see their discomfort affect mine, but not in a debilitating way
To see myself not take things personally, like the need for space
To see my gut telling me lies, losing connection to the trust that I should love myself as is
The emotional roller coaster is usually all my own doing (or undoing)

Chapter Six: A New Me
Growth only comes from an unraveling
I'm grateful it's happening
Like the scattering of my dad's ashes,
The moments we create are fleeting
I pledge to live in the now from now on
Grief took me through a process
A process which led to growth
This growth is a constant solving of problems...which may never be figured out
I accept that grey area
The new me won't try to control the outcome

wallflower against the party wall, staring at my own poems

one thing i notice i already mentioned:
what i know about eudaimonia is its name and general meaning
what's under the word i'm not familiar with

as to say i explored a philosophical theory without knowing about it
and since exploring theories is already problematic in its own way
conceptually speaking i was stacking problems on problems

but also this means that really overall
the poems sound and feel like me indeed
always now and then when i talk a problem out loud
all i hear is myself and what i already know
and i end up staying who i am, almost as if i like my imperfect self

sci-fi and punk were exaggerated in the autonomy portion
i realize now, later, for example
and some european philosopher recently reminded me that the
media is part of what robs us of our sense of autonomy
most eudaimonia sections i simply puzzled upon

these poems what they do is they echo my
continuous interior mysteries
my autonomy -- in some capacity there i know -- toward
walking through my internal hall of mirrors
toward and away from warped and wacky reflections of myself
within myself

indeed that's just me
which as i age well what i must do is accept who i am
alessandra's poems help me think about this, for sure

how much i like her poems, i'm glad to live with them and her
her as words, i keep reading, we keep writing
because what i know for sure is there are

the good people in the good fight and the spirit we need we have

We're Accepting Ourselves, And So That Makes Us Relate Positively With Each Other

A heavy weight has been lifted
It's like going to therapy on repeat

Feels better than everything, but
It took us everything to get here

Growth came from discomfort
It was horrible then lovely then horrible then lovely again

There'll be more discomfort so there'll be more growth
We're prepared to swim the horrible and lovely

Could be pretty murky, this swimming lifestyle
But through the murk, you get to the

Place you get to and there you are, you, who you've always been
Swimming next to another person (sometimes... like now)

Comfortable in our discomfort

More books for homes and hearts from

NEON BURRITO PUBLISHING

Basic Mutant Psychosis: Annals of Los Angeles 2014-2016

Stuck in an Elevator Between the 12th & 14th Floors of an Apartment Building on Rossmore

a Novel

by Morgan Drolet

www.ingramcontent.com/pod-product-compliance
Lightning Source LLC
Chambersburg PA
CBHW031401040426
42444CB00005B/380